GOD SPEAKS TO YOU

The Bible presented to young people

2.
THE NEW TESTAMENT

COLLINS

Collins Liturgical Publications
8 Grafton Street, London W1X 3LA

Distributed in Ireland by
Educational Company of Ireland
21 Talbot Street, Dublin

Collins Liturgical Australia
PO Box 3023, Sydney 2001

This introduction to the Bible was devised by
François Monfort, Daniel Perrot, François Louvel,
Isabelle-Marie Rioux, Dominique Huet and Marie-France Léna
Illustrations by Camille Bertholle-Duraz
Design by Jean-Marie Bertholle
Translated into English by Sarah Fawcett

English translation © William Collins Sons & Co Ltd
Bible text from Good News Bible, © American Bible Society, New York 1976

First published in French by Les Editions du Cerf, © 1985 Les Editions du Cerf
English edition, first published 1986
ISBN 0 00 599893 X

Photos: Araud: pp. 15, 21; Garnier: pp. 4, 5, 41, 49, 53, 73;
Giraudon: p. 85; Lagaillardie: end-papers; Tournus: pp. 11, 19, 23, 25, 27, 29, 31, 33,
35, 37, 39, 43, 45, 47, 51, 55, 57, 59, 61, 63, 65,
67, 69, 71, 77, 81, 83 86

Typeset by John Swain & Son Ltd, Glasgow
Printed in Spain

Contents

	page
This is a book about Jesus	4
A new covenant	6
About the map of Palestine	8
1 You shall call him Jesus *(Luke 1:26-38)*	10
2 A Saviour is born *(Luke 2:1-14)*	12
3 Prepare the way of the Lord *(Mark 1:1-18)*	14
4 You are my own dear Son *(Mark 1:9-13)*	16
5 He has sent me to preach the good news *(Luke 4:16-22)*	18
6 Follow me *(Mark 1:16-20)*	20
7 I have come to call sinners *(Matthew 9:9-13)*	22
8 Your sins are forgiven *(Mark 2:1-12)*	24
9 Is this allowed? *(Mark 3:1-6)*	26
10 You need only one thing *(From Mark 10)*	28
11 If you only knew what God gives! *(From John 4)*	30
12 Happy are those . . . *(Matthew 5:1-10)*	32
13 Our Father *(Matthew 6:6-13)*	34
14 Who is my neighbour? *(From Luke 10)*	36
15 My son was lost and has been found *(Luke 15:11-32)*	38
16 Then Jesus took bread *(John 6:1-15)*	40
17 I am the living bread *(From John 6)*	42
18 Who do you say I am? *(Matthew 16:13-21)*	44
19 Do not be afraid *(Matthew 17:1-9)*	46

	page
20 I must stay in your house today *(Luke 19:1-10)*	48
21 I am the resurrection and the life *(John 11:17-45)*	50
22 You did it for me *(Matthew 25:31-46)*	52
23 Take it, this is my body *(From Mark 14)*	54
24 He deserves to die *(From Mark 14 and 15)*	56
25 He who was crucified is risen! *(From Mark 15 and 16)*	58
26 Then their eyes were opened *(Luke 24:13-35)*	60
27 Stop your doubting and believe *(John 20:19-29)*	62
28 To the ends of the earth *(Acts 1:4-9)*	64
29 Filled with the Holy Spirit *(From Acts 2)*	66
30 They shared all they had *(Acts 2:41-47)*	68
31 In the name of Jesus Christ *(Acts 3:1-16; 4:1-3)*	70
32 Lord Jesus receive my spirit *(From Acts 6 and 8)*	72
33 I am Jesus whom you persecute *(Acts 9:1-12 . 17-20)*	74
34 Sent by the Holy Spirit *(From Acts 11 and 13)*	76
35 We will go to the Gentiles *(From Acts 13)*	78
36 Do this in memory of me *(1 Corinthians 11:17-18 . 20-26)*	80
37 You must try to be like him *(From Ephesians 4 and 5)*	82
38 Come, Lord Jesus *(Revelation 21:1-5)*	84
That our joy may be complete	86

This is a book about Jesus

Jesus is such an important person, that we calculate our dates from the year of his birth. This means that today it is nearly two thousand years since Jesus was living here on earth. So how do we know what he did? How do we know him?

First, people talked about Jesus

We know Jesus, because those who lived with him and became his friends talked about him. They declared that they had seen him alive after his death, that they had seen him risen from the dead. And that extraordinary event became the source of a tremendous new hope.

Others, who believed what these people said, came together and shared with one another as brothers and sisters. Soon people began to call them 'Christians' (from the Greek word *Christianos*) because they said that Jesus was the 'Christ' — that is the 'Messiah', the one awaited by the Jews who was to establish a kingdom of justice and peace. These communities of Christians called themselves the 'church' which means 'assembly'.

The first churches came into being in Jerusalem and in other parts of Palestine, the country of the Jews — it was Jesus' country too since he was a Jew. Then other churches were founded in the neighbouring countries — for example in Syria, at Damascus and Antioch. The twelve apostles, and above all a man called Paul who joined their company, undertook extensive journeys to make Jesus Christ known far and wide; these journeys led to churches being formed in the major cities and towns of the Near East and of Greece: Ephesus, Thessalonica, Corinth . . . and finally in Rome, the capital of the Roman Empire. In all these places the apostles and the others who went on these missions began by telling the good news of the resurrection of Jesus: they talked about him at length, telling the story of his life and passing on his teaching. To become a Christian you had to believe in Jesus, love him and strive to be like him. That meant that you really had to know him well. Everything said by eye-witnesses who had seen and heard Jesus was carefully listened to, committed to memory and told over and over again within the community.

Gradually, some of Jesus' sayings were written down, so that they would not be forgotten, and so that they could be handed on more reliably. What Jesus had said and what he had done was very precious to the first Christians. At the same time letters (*epistles*), written by the apostles to encourage the new Christians in their faith, began to circulate among the churches. Sometimes between 50 and 52 (some twenty years after Jesus' death) Paul wrote two letters to the Christians of Thessalonica; later he wrote to other communities: in Rome, Corinth, Ephesus . . . and to some of his personal friends. We possess a dozen or so of his letters. In about 64, Peter, the leader of the apostles, wrote a long epistle to all the churches.

When they came together to pray, the Christians loved to read out loud these letters from the apostles, as this helped them to believe more strongly.

Then the gospels were written down

After Peter's death, shortly before the year 70, **Mark** began recording the teachings of the apostles and gathering together those sayings of Jesus that had already been put down in writing. While he was doing this, he wrote a book for the church in Rome; this book gave an account of the person, the message and the mystery of Jesus. Mark's book is called a 'gospel', the word gospel means 'good news'. Who was Mark? You will find out on page 14.

Ten years late, Luke (*see page 10*) and Matthew (*see page 22*) wrote their gospels. **Luke** wrote especially for the Greek converts to Christ; and he followed it up with another book, *The Acts of the Apostles* which tells how first Peter and later Paul were led by the Holy Spirit to preach the good news to the 'pagans' (people who were not Jews). **Matthew** wrote especially for the Jewish Christians. His main aim was to explain how Jesus fulfilled what the prophets (God's spokesmen) had said.

The gospels of Mark, Luke and Matthew are similar in many ways, but they are not identical. There are two reasons for this: each writer put down in his own words what he knew about Jesus; and more importantly still, each of them was writing for a community that had its own life, its own questions and its own problems. **John's** gospel, written in Ephesus in about the year 90, expresses the thought of Christians who had had many years of reflection and prayer since the death and resurrection of Jesus. This fourth gospel helps us to get to know Jesus and his teaching even better.

The New Testament

During this period when the gospels were being written, and copied out and circulated among the churches, the apostles and other disciples wrote letters, as Paul had done, to feed and clarify the faith of the Christians. Among these letters are the Epistle to the Hebrews and the three epistles of John.

In 95, a great persecution was unleashed against the Christians. While it was going on a text was circulated among the churches. This was the Apocalypse of St John, which sought to sustain their courage and strengthen their hope with its assurance that the living Christ is and always will be present in his Church, whatever the dangers and dramas of history. The four gospels, the Acts of the Apostles, the twenty-one epistles and the Apocalypse together make up the New Testament, or Book of the New Covenant between God and the human race. It continues and completes the first covenant (the Old Testament). Together the Old and New Testaments form the Bible, the book of the Word of God. When you listen to a passage from the Bible being read out in church, or when you read it on your own, God speaks to you.

A new covenant

The Bible has two parts

— The first and longer of the two was written by the Jews, to whom God had revealed himself. They call it *The Torah*, that is *The Law* — the law of love on which their lives are centred. Christians call it *The Old Testament*, the *Old Covenant* or *First Covenant*.

— The second is concerned with the coming on earth of Jesus, the Son of God. It is the *New Testament* or *New Covenant*.

To help you discover the Bible for yourself, we have published two books

The one you are now beginning to read is *volume II;* it tells you about the new covenant brought to the human race by Jesus.

The first book (we shall call it *volume I:* remember this term; you are going to meet it again) corresponds to the first part of the Bible. It describes God's long, slow revelation of himself through the history of the people of Israel. It explains the role of the prophets, who were God's messengers. It speaks of the prayer of the Jews, above all as we find it in the psalms. It helps us to understand how the Jews were called by God to be his witnesses in the world, and how they responded to that call.

How the Bible came down to us

The oldest books of the Bible were passed on by word of mouth long before they were written down. An individual who, under the inspiration of the Holy Spirit, produced a story, a sermon or a prayer, would recite what he had thought up to other people, they in their turn would repeat it to others; and sometimes they went on telling it by word of mouth for centuries.

Later, when writing was discovered, some people were given the task of writing down these stories, sayings, histories and prayers. That's how it was done in Jesus' time, and for many centuries after, since printing was not invented until the fifteenth century. Before that time all books were written down by hand — which is why they are called 'manuscripts' (from the Latin *manus*= hand, *scribo*=I write).

The Old Testament, which was written in Hebrew, was translated into Greek round about the third and second centuries before Christ (BC). The New Testament was written in Greek during the first century after Christ (AD). The earliest known manuscripts of the Old Testament, date from the three centuries immediately before the birth of Christ; and the oldest manuscripts of the New Testament date from the third and fourth centuries AD.

Today the Bible has been translated into almost every language. No other book has spread so widely throughout the world.

The prophet Ezekiel, who lived seven centuries before Jesus, described some strange messengers of God which had four faces: one was the face of a man, another the face of a lion, the third was the face of a bull and the fourth the face of an eagle. Christians have taken up these images, applying to each of the four evangelists, who were also messengers of God, one of the symbols of which the ancient prophet spoke. The symbol of the man was given to Matthew, that of the lion to Mark, that of the bull to Luke and that of the eagle to John.
In painting and sculpture the evangelists are very often represented by their symbols. On this page you can see illuminations taken from old books of chants.

Manuscripts from Bildes (late twelfth and thirteenth centuries). Bibliothèque Sainte-Geneviève. Paris.

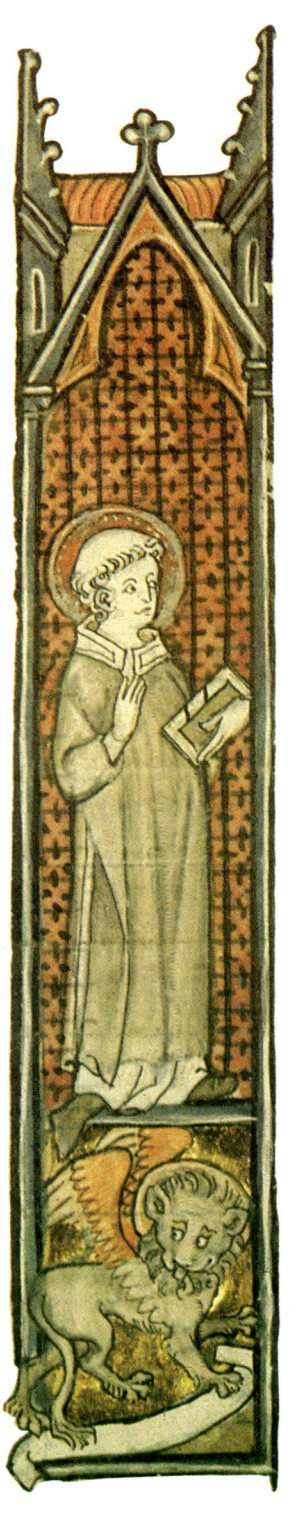

The Bible is 'the book'

(From the Greek word *biblos:* book)

It is the most important book of all, and different from all others. For the real author of the Bible is God.

27 books make up the New Testament

The gospel of St Matthew
The gospel of St Mark
The gospel of St Luke
The gospel of St John
The Acts of the Apostles
The epistles of St Paul:
— to the Romans
— to the Corinthians (two letters)
— to the Galatians
— to the Ephesians
— to the Philippians
— to the Colossians
— to the Thessalonians (two letters)
— to Timothy (two letters)
— to Titus
— to Philemon
The epistle to the Hebrews
The epistle of St James
The two epistles of St Peter
The three epistles of St John
The epistle of St Jude
The Apocalypse (Revelation)

In the Bible there are about 70 different books

Some are short, some are long. To make it easier for people to find their way around, the *books* have been divided into *chapters.* And within the chapters individual phrases or groups of phrases have been numbered — these are called *verses.*

You can tell where to look for a *quotation* (the particular passage you are discussing) in the Bible when you know its *reference;* that is when you know which book, which chapter and which verse to turn to. In this book the reference for the first passage is Luke 1:26-38. That means that it comes from the first chapter of St Luke's gospel, verses 26 to 38.

The Koran

This is the *Muslims'* sacred book. Many of the Old Testament prophets figure in it, notably Abraham, Moses, David and Elijah. The Koran does not recognise Jesus as the Son of God but sees him as a great prophet. It speaks of him, and of Mary his mother, with great respect.

The religion of the Muslims is called *Islam*. It was founded in the 7th century after the birth of Christ by the prophet *Mohammed*.

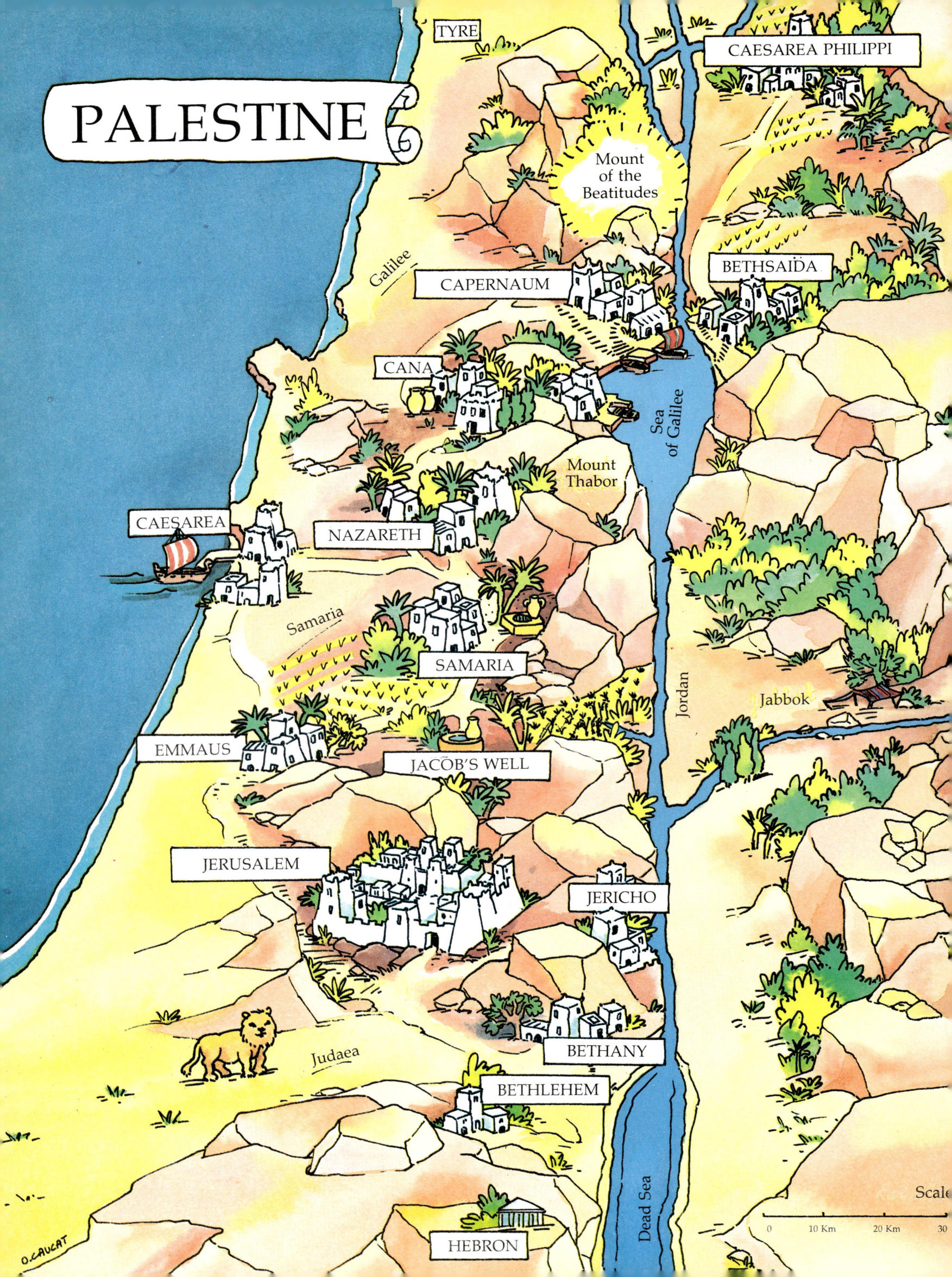

PALESTINE

- TYRE
- CAESAREA PHILIPPI
- Mount of the Beatitudes
- Galilee
- CAPERNAUM
- BETHSAIDA
- CANA
- Sea of Galilee
- Mount Thabor
- CAESAREA
- NAZARETH
- Samaria
- SAMARIA
- Jordan
- Jabbok
- EMMAUS
- JACOB'S WELL
- JERUSALEM
- JERICHO
- Judaea
- BETHANY
- BETHLEHEM
- Dead Sea
- HEBRON

Scale
0   10 Km   20 Km   30

About the map of Palestine

Look at the map of Palestine

The country lies at the easternmost end of the Mediterranean (see page 12). It is easy to travel quickly from north to south, a distance of less than two hundred kilometres. It is more difficult to get from east to west (an average distance of fifty kilometres) because you have to cross the mountain range that runs the length of the valley of the Jordan, the principal river. In the north there is a wide plain on which wheat, barley, fruit (pomegranates, figs and olives) and all sorts of vegetables are cultivated. On the hills, vines are grown. Up in the mountains, sheep and goats are raised.

Fish are caught in Lake Tiberias and in the Mediterranean Sea. In the south there is the Dead Sea, so called because it is so salty that no fish can live in it.

People used to travel round mainly on foot, using donkeys to carry heavy loads. It is very hot in summer, but in winter the temperature drops considerably and it sometimes snows in Jerusalem.

In Jesus' time the principal provinces of the country were Judea — which included the only large town, the capital Jerusalem — Samaria and Galilee.

Palestine was occupied by the Romans, to whom taxes had to be paid. The Romans were represented by a governor, but had left untouched the religious institutions of the Jews, which were very powerful. The High Priest was extremely important. He was responsible for worship in the Temple and was also leader of the Council — or Sanhedrin — and of the priests. All the priests served in the Temple in Jerusalem, since that was the only place where sacrifices were offered to God. In all the other towns, houses of prayer — known as synagogues — had been built.

Every aspect of people's lives was guided by religion. The word of God, studied by rabbis, scribes and doctors of the law, regulated every individual's daily life. It was the 'law' of the Jewish people.

1

You shall call him Jesus

Only Luke and Matthew
have passed on to us
an account
of the birth and childhood
of Jesus.
Luke, who was Greek, was a doctor.
He did not live in Palestine
and he never met Jesus.
A disciple and assistant
of the apostle Paul,
he accompanied him on his journeys,
notably those to Jerusalem,
Ephesus and Rome.
It is very likely
that Luke met Mary,
the mother of Jesus,
and was able to record her recollections.

Annunciation (anonymous). Icon Museum. Dubrovnik.

The encounter between the angel and Mary — known as the 'Annunciation' — takes place in Nazareth. Today this is an important town, but in those days it was only a village in the hills of Galilee. Few people lived there and those that did were quite poor. Their main concerns were their gardens, their fields and their flocks of sheep and goats. They had also built a little synagogue (house of prayer).

This encounter teaches us three things in particular.

1. The child whose birth is announced is the one promised by God to King David. God, speaking through the prophet Nathan, had told David 'You will always have descendants, and I will make your kingdom last forever. Your dynasty will never end.' The child is the Messiah for whom the people of Israel have been waiting (see volume 1, chapter 2): the descendant of David who will found the kingdom promised by God. And because he comes as a saviour, he will receive the name Jesus, which means 'God saves'.

2. Nothing is impossible for God: it is God's Spirit who initiates the life of Jesus within Mary. And for that reason she is an exceptional mother. But from that day on, for nine months, she carried her child inside her body, like all other mothers. In Mary, and through her, God became human.

3. In order that this extraordinary event might take place, Mary had to say 'yes' to the angel. She could not know in advance all that God would want of her, nor could she guess what the life and death of her son would be like. But she believed the message that had been given to her. She put her trust in the Lord.

²⁶In the sixth month of Elizabeth's pregnancy God sent the angel Gabriel to a town in Galilee named Nazareth. ²⁷He had a message for a girl promised in marriage to a man named Joseph, who was a descendant of King David. The girl's name was Mary. ²⁸The angel came to her and said, 'Peace be with you! The Lord is with you and has greatly blessed you!'

²⁹Mary was deeply troubled by the angel's message, and she wondered what his words meant. ³⁰The angel said to her, 'Don't be afraid, Mary; God has been gracious to you. ³¹You will become pregnant and give birth to a son, and you will name him Jesus. ³²He will be great and will be called the Son of the Most High God. The Lord God will make him a king, as his ancestor David was, ³³and he will be the king of the descendants of Jacob for ever; his kingdom will never end!'

³⁴Mary said to the angel, 'I am a virgin. How, then, can this be?'

³⁵The angel answered, 'The Holy Spirit will come on you, and God's power will rest upon you. For this reason the holy child will be called the Son of God. ³⁶Remember your relative Elizabeth. It is said that she cannot have children, but she herself is now six months pregnant, even though she is very old. ³⁷For there is nothing that God cannot do.'

³⁸'I am the Lord's servant,' said Mary; 'may it happen to me as you have said.' And the angel left her.

Luke 1:26-38

The words of the Angel Gabriel to Mary
are recalled in the opening lines of this prayer:

Hail Mary, full of grace.
The Lord is with thee.
Blessed art thou among women,
and blessed is the fruit of thy womb, Jesus.
Holy Mary, Mother of God,
pray for us sinners, now,
and at the hour of our death. Amen.

2

A Saviour is born to you

At this time,
the Roman Empire extended
from Spain to Iran
and from the North Sea
to the Sahara.
Palestine
was therefore part of it,
and it was an extremely
well-organised country.
Trade was flourishing
and the Roman army
maintained order and peace.
To distribute
the burden of taxation
more fairly,
the Emperor Augustus
ordered a census —
that is to say,
a listing
of all the inhabitants
of his empire.
It was at this point
that the Son of God
entered history,
almost two thousand years ago.

[1] **At that time the Emperor Augustus ordered a census to be taken throughout the Roman Empire.** [2] **When this first census took place, Quirinius was the governor of Syria.** [3] **Everyone, went to register himself, each to his own town.**
[4] **Joseph went from the town of Nazareth in Galilee to the town of Bethlehem in Judaea, the birthplace of King David. Joseph went there because he was a descendant of David.** [5] **He went to register with Mary, who was promised in marriage to him. She was pregnant,** [6] **and while they were in Bethlehem, the time came for her to have her baby.** [7] **She gave birth to her first son, wrapped him in strips of cloth and laid him in a manger — there was no room for them to stay in the inn.**
[8] **There were some shepherds in that part of the country who were spending the night in the fields, taking care of their flocks.** [9] **An angel of the Lord appeared to them, and the glory of the Lord shone over them. They were terribly afraid,** [10] **but the angel said to them, 'Don't be afraid! I am here with good news for you, which will bring great joy to all the people.** [11] **This very day in David's town your Saviour was born — Christ the Lord!** [12] **And this is what will prove it to you: you will find a baby wrapped in strips of cloth and lying in a manger.'**
[13] **Suddenly a great army of heaven's angels appeared with the angel, singing praises to God:**
[14] **'Glory to God in the highest heaven, and peace on earth to those with whom he is pleased!'**

Luke 2:1-14

Once the census had been ordered by the Emperor, Joseph and Mary set out for Bethlehem — a little town in Judaea, a few kilometres from Jerusalem — because it was necessary to enrol in the town from which one's family came. David, Joseph's ancestor, was born in Bethlehem, and it is there too that Jesus is born. He will come to be called the 'Son of David' — a name often used in the gospels to make it clear that he is the Messiah promised by God and awaited by the people of Israel.

Jesus' birth is first announced, by the Angel of the Lord, to the shepherds; men who live a rough and simple life looking after their animals in the fields. The 'good news' (which is what the word 'gospel' means) was thus given first of all to the poor, for they have a greater need than others to know that God loves them.

The shepherds are told how to recognize the Messiah. He is a newborn child wrapped in swaddling clothes and laid in a manger — a trough for animals. A baby cannot survive unless it is cared for, fed and loved. That is how the Son of God reveals himself: frail and powerless. At a time when the Roman Empire is at the height of its splendour, God reveals himself not in the midst of human greatness and achievements but in littleness and poverty.

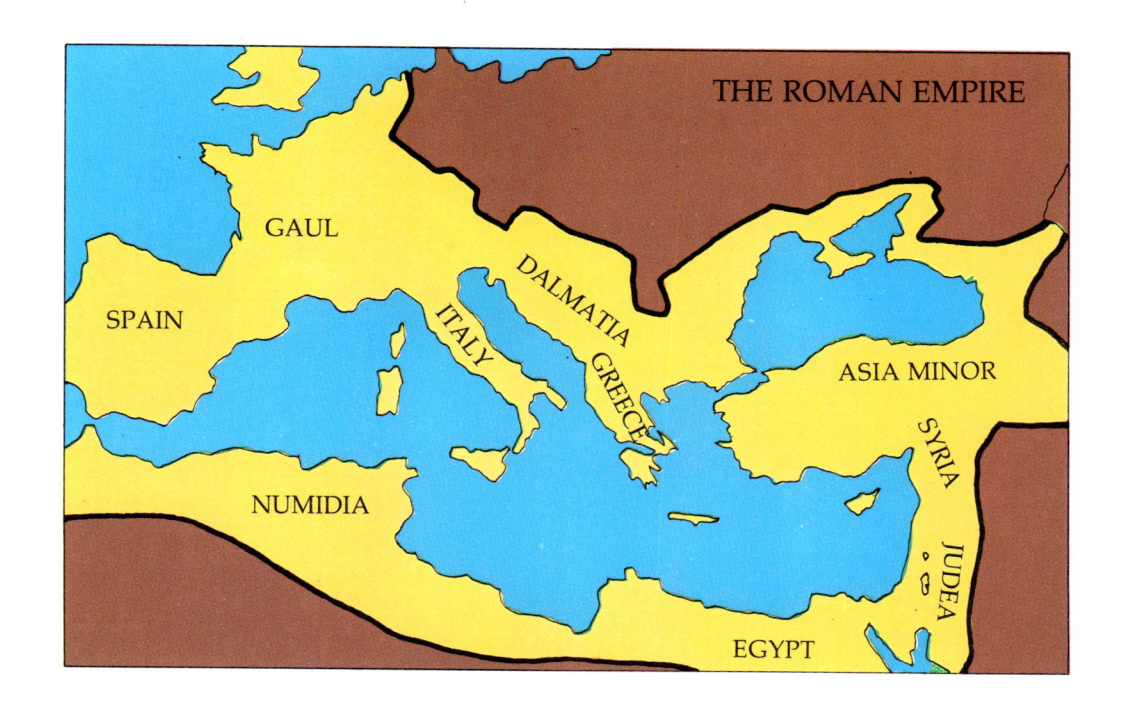

In Jesus the Son of God became man so that every human being might become a child of God. Jesus is as truly a child as any other . . . and he is God! This is the mystery of the Incarnation: Jesus is a man and that man is God. In this mystery God reveals to us just how much he loves human beings; he comes to share their life so that they in turn can share his.

*The joyous message
given to the shepherds
by the angels
is heard
in the following prayer.*

*Glory to God in the highest,
and peace on earth
to all people
for they are God's friends.
We praise you,
we bless you,
we adore you,
we glorify you,
we give you thanks
for your great glory.*

3 Prepare the way of the Lord

Mark came from Jerusalem,
and when he was young he probably met Jesus.
He accompanied first Paul and then Peter
on their great journeys.
His gospel, which was written in Rome,
passes on to us what the apostle Peter
said about Jesus.
It also shows the faith
of the Christians of Rome
in Jesus, Messiah and Son of God.
Mark begins his account by explaining the role
and the mission of John the Baptist.

¹This is the Good News about Jesus Christ, the Son of God. ²It began as the prophet Isaiah had written:
'God said, "I will send my messenger ahead of you to clear the way for you."'
³Someone is shouting in the desert,
'Get the road ready for the Lord;
make a straight path for him to travel!'
⁴So John appeared in the desert, baptizing and preaching. 'Turn away from your sins and be baptized,' he told the people, 'and God will forgive your sins.' ⁵Many people from the province of Judaea and the city of Jerusalem went out to hear John. They confessed their sins, and he baptized them in the River Jordan.
⁶John wore clothes made of camel's hair, with a leather belt round his waist, and his food was locusts and wild honey. ⁷He announced to the people, 'The man who will come after me is much greater than I am. I am not good enough to bend down and untie his sandals. ⁸I baptize you with water, but he will baptize you with the Holy Spirit.'

Mark 1:1-8

The Jordan in springtime,
seen from the bridge
of the Daughters of Jacob.

John, who is known as the Baptist (the 'baptizer'), was Jesus' cousin. He was born six months before Jesus. His parents, Elizabeth and Zechariah, had been unable to have children and had given up hope of having any because they were old; and yet, with God's help, they gave birth to this boy.

When he is about thirty, John, who lives in the desert near the Jordan, begins to speak about God. People come to find him because they believe he is a prophet, a man of prayer who is close to God and who speaks in his name. They begin gathering round him in greater and greater numbers.

John's mission is to be the 'precursor' — that is, the 'one who runs ahead' to announce the impending arrival of someone important. He proclaims that very soon the long-awaited Messiah will come among his people. John himself is self-effacing; he makes way for Jesus, who is about to make himself known.

To prepare themselves to greet the Messiah, John urges his disciples to give up their sins and turn towards God. As a sign of repentance he suggests that they immerse themselves in the River Jordan. Water cleanses and purifies and in the scorching heat of the desert it restores a person's energy; it is a sign of renewal.

John also says that the Messiah himself will baptize with the Holy Spirit. This had been announced in a veiled way as much as six centuries earlier by the prophet Ezekiel, when he said: 'I will put my spirit in you . . . and then you will live' (see volume 1, chapter 24).

The words 'baptize' and 'baptism' come from Greek words meaning 'to plunge into water' and 'bath'. To baptize is not to give something a name (as when we talk of 'baptizing a ship'), nor is it to undergo an experience that tests one's courage and strength for the first time (as in the expression a 'baptism of fire'). When people are baptized they are plunged into water in order to purify them from their sins and cause a new life to well up within them.

*When Christians meet in church today,
they may say, following John the Baptist:*

*Let us prepare to meet the Lord
by calling to mind our sins.
Let us say wholeheartedly:
I confess to God almighty
and to you my brothers and sisters,
that I have sinned, in my thoughts and in my words,
in what I have done and in what I have failed to do.*

4 You are my own dear Son

> ⁹Not long afterwards Jesus came from Nazareth in the province of Galilee, and was baptized by John in the Jordan. ¹⁰As soon as Jesus came up out of the water, he saw heaven opening and the Spirit coming down on him like a dove. ¹¹And a voice came from heaven, 'You are my own dear Son. I am pleased with you.'
>
> ¹²At once the Spirit made him go into the desert, ¹³where he stayed forty days, being tempted by Satan. Wild animals were there also, but angels came and helped him.
>
> *Mark 1:9-13*

Though he was born in Bethlehem,
Jesus spent the next thirty years
at Nazareth in Galilee,
where Joseph and Mary lived.
It was there that he grew up,
played with his friends,
prayed, at home with his family
and in the synagogue,
studied the Bible,
helped Joseph, a carpenter,
in the workshop,
and carried on his trade
among the people in the village.
He was a boy like any other.
And then one day he left.
The time had come
for him to begin his mission.
Before telling the people
about the kingdom of God,
he went to see John the Baptist
on the banks of the Jordan.

When we were baptized, God said to us as he did to Jesus: 'You are my beloved child.' On the day of our baptism the Father adopts us and gives us his life.

Do you know where and when you were baptized? Have you ever asked your parents why they had you baptized?

These five verses from St Mark's gospel tell us a great deal:

Jesus comes to be baptized. But why? Does he need to, in order to purify himself? The answer is that he does not, since he has committed no sin. However, by doing so he shows us that he is the brother of sinners: that he wants to be a man with other human beings.

As he comes out of the water, Jesus sees the Spirit coming down upon him — the Spirit who came upon David when he was anointed king, the Spirit who inspired the prophets to speak in the name of God, the Spirit through whom Jesus was conceived in the body of the Virgin Mary. This is the Spirit of God, the Holy Spirit.

So Jesus is not simply immersed in water, he is also taken over by the Spirit. He is baptized both in water and the Spirit. Water alone is only a sign. It is the Spirit that actually transforms. Later Jesus will say that in order to enter the kingdom of God, that is to share in God's life, it is necessary to be reborn of water and the Spirit.

Present at the time of Jesus' baptism therefore, are: the Father, whose voice is heard; Jesus, who is identified as the Son; and the Spirit, who unites them in love. Such is the mystery of God. And it explains why Christians are baptized 'in the name of the Father, and of the Son, and of the Holy Spirit'.

After his baptism, Jesus is led by the Spirit into the desert. He stays there for forty days, alone and in silence, in order to pray to his Father and to think about his mission. But even at this stage he has to confront Satan, the devil, (see volume I, chapter 15), who is trying to lead him astray from the path of loyalty to God. From now on, until his death, Jesus must fight against evil.

[5] He has sent me to preach the good news

Saturday, the Sabbath day,
is set aside for the Lord.
On this day Jews do not work.
They come together in the synagogue,
where they pray, using hymns and psalms.
They also read passages from the Bible;
a commentary is provided by the rabbi
(the teacher in the synagogue)
or by anyone who asks his permission
to provide one.

The first part of the Eucharist,
known as the 'liturgy of the Word',
adopts the same procedure.

¹⁶**Then Jesus went to Nazareth, where he had been brought up, and on the Sabbath he went as usual to the synagogue. He stood up to read the Scriptures ¹⁷and was handed the book of the prophet Isaiah. He unrolled the scroll and found the place where it was written,**
¹⁸**'The Spirit of the Lord is upon me,**
   because he has chosen me to bring
      good news to the poor.
He has sent me to proclaim liberty to the captives
   and recovery of sight to the blind;
to set free the oppressed
   ¹⁹**and announce that the time has come**
   when the Lord will save his people.'
   ²⁰**Jesus rolled up the scroll, gave it back to the attendant, and sat down. All the people in the synagogue had their eyes fixed on him, ²¹as he said to them, 'This passage of scripture has come true today, as you heard it being read.'**
   ²²**They were all well impressed with him and marvelled at the eloquent words that he spoke.**

Luke 4:16-22

During the feast of Passover. Presentation of the Torah (the Law). Scrolls dating from the Middle Ages.

One Sabbath day Jesus enters the synagogue where he has come so often and where he is known as the carpenter, the son of Joseph and Mary. He reads a passage from the Bible. It is the passage in which Isaiah explained the role of a messenger of God, of a Messiah. The prophet was talking about his own mission, but the Jews who read the text in the centuries that followed came to regard it as a description of the expected Messiah. When Jesus reads the passage aloud in the synagogue in Nazareth, he declares that on that very day the words of Isaiah have come true.

The event which occurred at the moment of his baptism (chapter 4) shows clearly that the Spirit of God is with Jesus: he is the Messiah (this is the Hebrew word), the Christ (in Greek *Christos*), 'the anointed One' (see volume I, chapter 10). Jesus has not been anointed with oil but directly with the power of the Holy Spirit. He has been consecrated to proclaim a kingdom of justice, peace and brotherhood: the kingdom of God. He has been sent to bring this good news to the poor, the imprisoned, the blind, the oppressed.

The poor are not only those who lack money, but also those who lack work, health, friends, hope. The imprisoned include, together with those men and women who are shut away in prisons and concentration camps, those who are the prisoners of their own habits, their own ideas. The blind are those whose eyes cannot see, but they are also those whose hearts and minds need opening to God's love. The oppressed include any who are treated unjustly, tortured or persecuted, in body or mind.

Jesus came to bring reconciliation, liberation and hope to all of them.

Today, once again, we hear the good news. Do you realise that it is addressed to everyone? God uses us as his messengers to the poor and the unhappy. You can give joy to those you meet, and share with them this good news: God loves them.

6
Follow me

After his baptism and his time in the desert
Jesus stopped living in Nazareth.
He moved around Galilee
proclaiming the good news
of the kingdom of God.
People began to recognize him
and to listen to him.
Jesus often went to the Sea of Galilee
(also known as Lake Tiberias).
There he met many fishermen,
and it was from among these fishermen
that he chose his first companions.

By the shore of Lake Tiberias in the evening.

> [16] As Jesus walked along the shore of Lake Galilee, he saw two fishermen, Simon and his brother Andrew, catching fish with a net. [17] Jesus said to them, 'Come with me, and I will teach you to catch men.' [18] At once they left their nets and went with him.
>
> [19] He went a little farther on and saw two other brothers, James and John, the sons of Zebedee. They were in their boat getting their nets ready. [20] As soon as Jesus saw them, he called them; they left their father Zebedee in the boat with the hired men and went with Jesus.
>
> *Mark 1:16-20*

---

*I thank you Lord Jesus,
for having made me your disciple
and your friend.
Help me to walk in your footsteps
with courage and confidence.
Thank you for making me a Christian:
for being my light and my joy.*

The fishermen Simon, Andrew, James and John are the first to follow Jesus, to take him as their master and to want to live with him. To be a disciple of Jesus is to be called by him and to follow him. As he himself will say later: 'You did not choose me; I chose you.'

The first person ever to be called by God to set out on a journey, was Abraham, nearly four thousand years ago (see volume I, chapter 12). Abraham left his country and his family in obedience to God, without knowing where this would take him. In the same way the Virgin Mary, when she said 'yes' to the angel of the Lord, did not understand what was going to happen to her. And when Simon and Andrew, James and John set out, they did not have any clear idea of where Jesus was leading them. They trusted him. They believed in him.

Once Jesus began to move from town to town preaching the good news, he invited individuals to accompany him and help him with his mission. Some followed him and so became his disciples. From among these disciples he picks twelve, who become known as 'apostles', that is 'messengers'. The twelve are Simon, whom he calls Peter, Andrew his brother, James and John the sons of Zebedee, Philip, Bartholomew, Matthew, Thomas, James son of Alphaeus, Simon 'the Zealot', Jude the brother of James, and Judas Iscariot, the one who later betrays Jesus.

In order to set out with Jesus, the first apostles left their boats and their nets behind them. Jesus told them that they would become 'fishers of men'. No longer will they catch fish, instead they will lead many men and women to the Lord.

7 I have come to call sinners

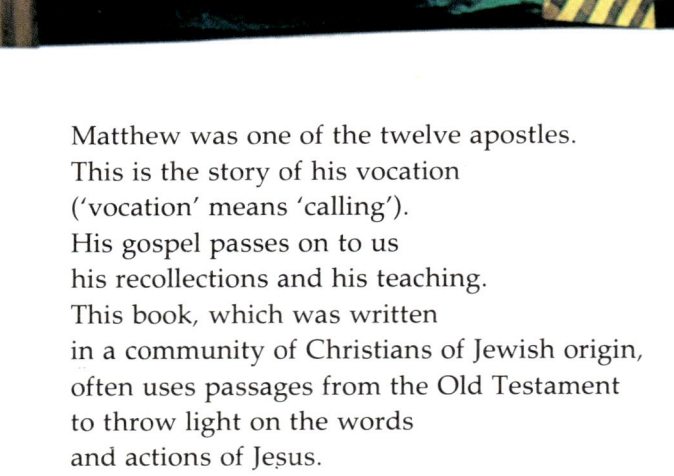

Matthew was one of the twelve apostles.
This is the story of his vocation
('vocation' means 'calling').
His gospel passes on to us
his recollections and his teaching.
This book, which was written
in a community of Christians of Jewish origin,
often uses passages from the Old Testament
to throw light on the words
and actions of Jesus.

⁹Jesus left that place, and as he walked along, he saw a tax collector, named Matthew, sitting in his office. He said to him, 'Follow me.'
Matthew got up and followed him.
¹⁰While Jesus was having a meal in Matthew's house, many tax collectors and other outcasts came and joined Jesus and his disciples at the table. ¹¹Some Pharisees saw this and asked his disciples, 'Why does your teacher eat with such people?'
¹²Jesus heard them and answered, 'People who are well do not need a doctor, but only those who are sick. ¹³Go and find out what is meant by the scripture that says: "It is kindness that I want, not animal sacrifices." I have not come to call respectable people, but outcasts.'

Matthew 9:9-13

The tax collectors were Jews who collected the taxes paid to the Emperor. The Roman administration required them to hand over to it a fixed sum in advance. The tax collectors took advantage of this, demanding more from their fellow townspeople and keeping the extra for themselves. They were regarded as thieves, and also as bad Jews, since they collaborated with the pagan occupiers of their country.

Matthew was a tax collector in Capernaum. Jesus invites Matthew to follow him. And Matthew replies 'yes', just as Simon, Andrew, James and John have done. He leaves his desk immediately. And, happy to set out with Jesus, he invites him to his house for a meal. Matthew also asks his friends, the other tax collectors in the town, to the meal.

The pharisees were Jews who strove to observe all the prescriptions of the Law, plus those that had been added by custom or tradition. Tradition forbade Jews to work for the pagans, and it regulated the details of what happened at mealtimes. So, when Jesus goes to eat with the tax collectors the pharisees are indignant, saying accusingly: 'He is a sinner, since he is sharing a meal with sinners.' In this way a conflict begins between Jesus and the pharisees, which will become more and more intense.

Jesus answers the pharisees accusation by saying that he has come precisely to call sinners and to heal their sickness. Sinners are like the paralysed, the blind or those afflicted by leprosy. They must be looked after and given treatment. Jesus therefore, does not hesitate to go to their homes, just as a doctor goes to the homes of the sick. As for the pharisees, they are satisfied with themselves as they are, and believe they have no need of help or healing.

Jesus recalls something said by the prophet Hosea: 'I want your constant love not your animal sacrifices.' God prefers mercy (forgiveness, love of others) to the ritual worship offered to him. Hosea's reproach to the Jews of his time can also be applied to the pharisees, who choose to observe the traditions rather than to love.

Throughout his life, Jesus will show mercy and urge sinners to become reconciled with the Father. And many will do so, like Matthew, who was to become St Matthew, the messenger of the Gospel.

Coin dating from the time of King Herod. It represents the table of offerings.

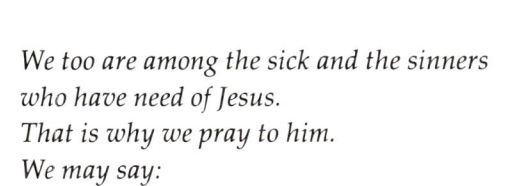

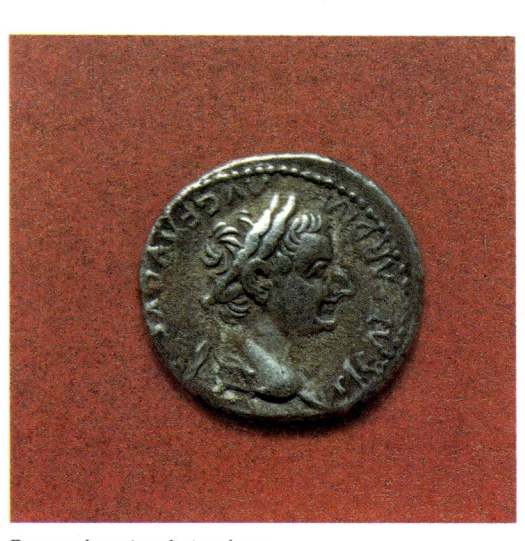

Roman denarius dating from the time of Tiberius Augustus (first century).

We too are among the sick and the sinners
who have need of Jesus.
That is why we pray to him.
We may say:

Lord Jesus, sent by the Father
to heal and save all men and women,
have mercy on us.
O Christ, you came into the world
to call all sinners,
have mercy on us.

8 Your sins are forgiven

During Jesus' lifetime
Capernaum
was one of the principal towns
on the shores of Lake Tiberias.
It was a fishing port.
Today
there are important ruins
in the area.
Archaeological digs
have led to the discovery
of the remains of the synagogue
and of many small houses
in the narrow streets
near the port.
It is very likely
that one of these houses
was the home of Simon Peter,
in which Jesus often stayed.

¹A few days later Jesus went back to Capernaum, and the news spread that he was at home. ²So many people came together that there was no room left, not even out in front of the door. Jesus was preaching the message to them ³when four men arrived, carrying a paralysed man to Jesus. ⁴Because of the crowd, however, they could not get the man to him. So they made a hole in the roof right above the place where Jesus was. When they had made an opening, they let the man down, lying on his mat. ⁵Seeing how much faith they had, Jesus said to the paralysed man, 'My son, your sins are forgiven.'

⁶Some teachers of the Law who were sitting there thought to themselves, ⁷'How does he dare to talk like this? This is blasphemy! God is the only one who can forgive sins!'

⁸At once Jesus knew what they were thinking, so he said to them, 'Why do you think such things? ⁹Is it easier to say to this paralysed man, "Your sins are forgiven", or to say, "Get up, pick up your mat, and walk"? ¹⁰I will prove to you, then, that the Son of Man has authority on earth to forgive sins.' So he said to the paralysed man, ¹¹'I tell you, get up, pick up your mat, and go home!'

¹²While they all watched, the man got up, picked up his mat, and hurried away. They were all completely amazed and praised God, saying, 'We have never seen anything like this!'

Mark 2:1-12

Modern Palestinian house constructed in the ancient manner, with a roof of boughs and clay.

Jesus has explained to the pharisees that he has come to heal the sick and reconcile sinners to God. That is his mission, foretold by the name that was given him when his birth was announced: 'Jesus', 'which means 'God saves'.

One day, in spite of the crowd surrounding the house, a paralysed man lying on a stretcher is brought to Jesus. The sick man does not ask for anything, though he certainly hopes to recover the use of his limbs. However, Jesus says nothing to him about that, instead he says to him, 'Your sins are forgiven.' Jesus goes straight to what is essential. He frees this man from a sickness even more serious than his paralysis: his sins. But among those who are looking on are some scribes (people who study the Bible), who are scandalized. They consider that Jesus has blasphemed — insulted God — by putting himself in God's place. In fact only God can forgive sins, since to sin is to disobey him, to offend him, to separate oneself from him.

Yes, God alone can forgive sins, just as he alone can, by his word, restore strength to the limbs of a paralytic. And so, as a sign of the forgiveness he brings and of the peace and love that he reawakens, Jesus tells the paralysed man to get up and walk. The healing of the body is the sign of another kind of healing, the healing of the heart.

By this gesture Jesus showed that he was acting in the name of God, and even suggested that he was God himself.

When the sacrament of reconciliation is administered to a sinner who is asking God's forgiveness, the sinner is told in the name of Jesus: 'Your sins are forgiven.' And in a way the sinner is also told: 'Get up and walk, go home and take up your life with courage and confidence, for the Lord is with you, and he loves you.'

9 Is this allowed?

Jesus disturbs people
who have fixed ideas about God,
about religion and holiness,
and about how we should live.
Thus the pharisees are furious
when he asserts that God prefers mercy
to literal observance of the commandments
(as we have seen in chapter 7),
or when he forgives sin (chapter 8).
Jesus' enemies are prepared to do anything
to silence him.
They spy on him,
looking for an excuse to accuse him
and if possible to get him condemned
in a court of law.

¹Then Jesus went back to the synagogue, where there was a man who had a paralysed hand. ²Some people were there who wanted to accuse Jesus of doing wrong; so they watched him closely to see whether he would heal the man on the Sabbath. ³Jesus said to the man, 'Come up here to the front.' ⁴Then he asked the people, 'What does our Law allow us to do on the Sabbath? To help or to harm? To save a man's life or to destroy it?'

But they did not say a thing. ⁵Jesus was angry as he looked round at them, but at the same time he felt sorry for them, because they were so stubborn and wrong. Then he said to the man, 'Stretch out your hand.' He stretched it out, and it became well again. ⁶So the Pharisees left the synagogue . . . and made plans to kill Jesus.

Mark 3:1 . . . 6

In the gospels Jesus does not say, 'this is allowed, that is forbidden'. He calls people to love and shows by his life what that means: he is respectful of others, attentive to each individual and courageous in the face of opposition and threats.

Detail of *The Resurrection of Christ*. Germain Pilon. The Louvre.

In Jewish eyes the law of the Sabbath is sacred. On that day, the Lord's Day, all work and all exertion are forbidden. Tradition has increased the number of prohibitions: for instance, it is forbidden to light a fire or to walk more than one thousand paces. Jesus knows that the law of the Sabbath, laid down by Moses, comes from God (see volume I, chapter 6). However he also knows that every law coming from God is meant to be at the service of love. He is not afraid to say so in the synagogue.

At the synagogue, Jesus tells a sick man in the crowd to come forward into the middle, in front of everyone. Then he asks: 'What does our Law allow us to do on the Sabbath? To help or to harm? To save a man's life or destroy it?' It is a trick question: no one can reply that we are allowed to do harm or to kill! But it is a question that forces them to think. Does God want to tie people down to laws that have been established once and for all, regulating what is allowed and what is forbidden? Or does he want to open up their hearts to love; to free them from all hardness and rigidity?

Jesus teaches those who listen to him that the Law of Love is 'his commandment'. This commandment thrusts aside all permissions and prohibitions, for no law should forbid healing or saving. To minister to someone who has suffered misfortune, to help someone who needs to be helped, to care for someone who is sick — or in other words to love — is what really matters. Which is why, on this Sabbath day, Jesus cures the paralysed hand of the sick man. On another occasion he said: 'The Sabbath was made for man, not man for the Sabbath.' This means that human beings are the most important thing; the law of the Sabbath was intended not to make slaves of people but to give them time to spend with God and to rest a little.

10

You need only one thing

In this passage
Mark speaks several times
of Jesus' facial expression:
his expression of love
for the man
who has sought him out,
of sadness
at the man's negative response,
of authority
when he teaches the apostles.
The gospel often mentions
how Jesus uses eye contact.
This ensures his encounters
are real encounters.
And he leaves each of us
free to say yes or no.

¹⁷As Jesus was starting on his way again, a man ran up, knelt before him, and asked him, 'Good Teacher, what must I do to receive eternal life?' . . .

¹⁸Jesus said to him. ¹⁹'You know the commandments: "Do not commit murder; do not commit adultery; do not steal; do not accuse anyone falsely; do not cheat; respect your father and your mother."'

²⁰'Teacher,' the man said, 'ever since I was young, I have obeyed all these commandments.'

²¹Jesus looked straight at him with love and said, 'You need only one thing. Go and sell all you have and give the money to the poor, and you will have riches in heaven; then come and follow me.' ²²When the man heard this, gloom spread over his face, and he went away sad, because he was very rich.

²³Jesus looked round at his disciples and said to them, 'How hard it will be for rich people to enter the Kingdom of God!' . . . ²⁶At this the disciples were completely amazed and asked one another, 'Who, then, can be saved?'

²⁷Jesus looked straight at them and answered, 'This is impossible for man, but not for God; everything is possible for God.'

Mark 10:17 . 19-23 . 26-27

Ancient stained glass window.

A man full of good intentions asks Jesus what he should do. Jesus begins by telling him to live according to the commandments of God. Then he makes a personal appeal. The man needs to do 'only one thing', Jesus says, in order to commit himself totally to the Lord. He must give up his fortune, his comforts, his business concerns.

We cannot do without money: we need it to live. But money is dangerous, because many people think only about how to make more of it, and so have no time left for prayer or for other people. Money is their idol. Jesus says: 'No one can be a slave of two masters . . . you cannot serve God and money.' Anyone who loves money too much does not love God enough. Jesus asks all of us to ensure that we do not become enslaved by money. In addition, he asks some people to give up everything in order to follow him.

When Jesus called Simon, Andrew, James and John, the fishermen, and Matthew, the tax collector, they set out with him, leaving behind all they had. Giving up their livelihood and their security, they followed Jesus because they trusted him. But this man, to whom Jesus said: 'Sell all you have and give the money to the poor; . . . then come and follow me', is very rich. He is attached to his fortune and cannot bring himself to give it up. He is unhappy about this, but he goes away. Jesus too is sad. He explains to his disciples: it is difficult for someone who is rich to enter the Kingdom of God! It is difficult for someone who has a lot of money to keep his heart free and receptive, so that he can live like Jesus.

To give up everything seems hard to do. But God fills the hearts of certain people with enough love to enable them to do it. That is why there have always been, and still are, men and women, even among the very rich, who give up everything and make themselves poor in order to follow Jesus.

The gospel is the only true form of riches on which we can safely build our lives.

11

If you only knew what God gives!

On the map of Palestine (page 8) you can see that Samaria is situated in the middle of the country, between Galilee in the north and Judea (with the capital, Jerusalem) in the south. Because the inhabitants of Samaria have built themselves a rival temple to the Temple in Jerusalem, the Jews regard them as false friends who do not follow the true religion. They detest and despise them. However Jesus detests and despises no one. He unhesitatingly enters into conversation with a Samaritan woman, who is very surprised that he should do so. She will be even more surprised as she listens to his words, which will convert and transform her.

⁵In Samaria he came to a town named Sychar, which was not far from the field that Jacob had given to his son Joseph. ⁶Jacob's well was there, and Jesus, tired out by the journey, sat down by the well. It was about noon.

⁷A Samaritan woman came to draw some water, and Jesus said to her, 'Give me a drink of water.' (⁸His disciples had gone into town to buy food.)

⁹The woman answered, 'You are a Jew, and I am a Samaritan — so how can you ask me for a drink?' (Jews will not use the same cups and bowls that Samaritans use.)

¹⁰Jesus answered, 'If only you knew what God gives and who it is that is asking you for a drink, you would ask him, and he would give you life-giving water.'

¹¹'Sir,' the woman said, 'you haven't got a bucket, and the well is deep. Where would you get that life-giving water? ¹²It was our ancestor Jacob who gave us this well; he and his sons and his flocks all drank from it. You don't claim to be greater than Jacob, do you?'

¹³Jesus answered, 'Whoever drinks this water will be thirsty again, ¹⁴but whoever drinks the water that I will give him will never be thirsty again. The water that I will give him will become in him a spring which will provide him with life-giving water and give him eternal life.'

¹⁵'Sir,' the woman said, 'give me that water! Then I will never be thirsty again, nor will I have to come here to draw water.'

¹⁶'Go and call your husband,' Jesus told her, 'and come back.'

¹⁷'I haven't got a husband,' she answered.

Jesus replied, 'You are right when you say you haven't got a husband. ¹⁸You have been married to five men, and the man you live with now is not really your husband. You

Woman by a well in Samaria.

have told me the truth.'

¹⁹'I see you are a prophet, sir,' the woman said. ²⁰'My Samaritan ancestors worshipped God on this mountain, but you Jews say that Jerusalem is the place where we should worship God.'

²¹Jesus said to her, 'Believe me, woman, the time will come when people will not worship the Father either on this mountain or in Jerusalem. ²³But the time is coming and is already here, when by the power of God's Spirit people will worship the Father as he really is, offering him the true worship that he wants. ²⁴God is Spirit, and only by the power of his Spirit can people worship him as he really is.'

²⁵The woman said to him, 'I know that the Messiah will come, and when he comes, he will tell us everything.'

²⁶Jesus answered, 'I am he, I who am talking with you.'

²⁷At that moment Jesus' disciples returned, and they were greatly surprised to find him talking with a woman. But none of them said to her, 'What do you want?' or asked him, 'Why are you talking with her?'

²⁸Then the woman left her water jar, went back to the town, and said to the people there, ²⁹'Come and see the man who told me everything I have ever done. Could he be the Messiah?' ³⁰So they left the town and went to Jesus . . .

⁴⁰So when the Samaritans came to him, they begged him to stay with them, and Jesus stayed there two days. ⁴¹Many more believed because of his message, ⁴²and they said to the woman, 'We believe now, not because of what you said, but because we ourselves have heard him, and we know that he really is the Saviour of the world.'

John 4:5-30 . 41-42

In the course of this long conversation, Jesus and the Samaritan woman talk about her life and her husbands; Jesus finds that she has been unhappy with all her husbands. He helps her to discover some essential truths:

God is the source of life. Fresh water, flowing water, is the stuff of dreams for people who live in dry countries like Palestine. The first thoughts that come into the woman's mind as she listens to Jesus are that she might never be thirsty again, or tire herself out walking to the well. But there is something else that Jesus wants her to understand: that in the human heart there is a thirst far greater than any bodily thirst. This thirst is the need we all have for hope, joy, peace and love, a thirst which only God can quench.

God asks those who worship him to do so in spirit and in truth. Jesus does not reject the Temple in Jerusalem (on the contrary he often goes there to pray and teach). What he does say is that it is not the place where we worship God that is most important, but the way in which we worship him. To pray 'in spirit and in truth' means to be honest in one's prayer and not simply to go through the motions.

Jesus is the Messiah. As she listens to him, the Samaritan woman realises that this is no ordinary man but a spokesman for God, a prophet. Jesus is planning to reveal to her who he is: when the woman says she is waiting for the Messiah who will bring the light, Jesus replies: 'I am he.' This woman, who so needs to be saved, is filled with wonder at this good news. She is unable to keep it to herself, and runs off at once to look for her friends and neighbours. They too, having heard what Jesus has to say, believe in him. 'He really is the Saviour of the world,' they say.

As a deer longs for cool water,
so I long for you, O God.
I thirst for you, the living God;
when can I worship in your presence?
I will put my hope in God, and praise him,
He is my Saviour and my God.
(Psalm 41)

12 Happy are those who...

On Mount Sinai
Moses received from God
the ten commandments,
which sum up
the law of the old covenant.
The Jews had to obey them
if they wanted to be faithful
to their Lord.
On a mountain in Galilee,
Jesus promulgates the law
of the new covenant.
This begins with
eight conditions for happiness,
according to the heart of God.
These are the 'Beatitudes'.
They are full of surprises.

God created human beings to be happy. On one of the first occasions that Jesus speaks to the crowds, he proclaims and promises happiness. But what exactly is happiness? It means having a heart open to love; it means living with God. People are happy when they succeed in bringing out what is best in themselves — when they love, when they share, when they spread happiness, even if giving means depriving themselves. The achievement of something difficult and noble brings happiness. Being inwardly free, and not at the mercy of one's whims brings happiness.

The happiness Jesus describes is his own happiness: the Beatitudes express the secret of his own life. He is humble, gentle, and merciful; he is a peacemaker, he is persecuted . . . and he lives fully, both as a human being and as Son of God. He is filled with love, he is happy!

Following Jesus means committing oneself to a difficult path, but that path leads to true joy. People often say: happy are those who are rich, strong, powerful; happy are those who have many possessions, those who wield power over others. Jesus on the other hand, says: happy are those who are not attached to riches, who do not use violent means to obtain and hang on to what they want; they are open to love and their hearts will be filled. Happy are those whose hearts are pure, who shun what is false, self-seeking and cowardly: they will know the joy of God. Happy are those who struggle for justice and peace, happy even if they are persecuted: God will open the doors of his Kingdom to them.

The Beatitudes, which reveal Jesus and his message, also reveal to individual men and women what they are, and what they must do to be happy. God, who created human beings out of love, offers them this happiness.

¹Jesus saw the crowds and went up a hill, where he sat down. His disciples gathered round him, ²and he began to teach them:
³'Happy are those who know they are spiritually poor;
    the Kingdom of heaven belongs to them!
⁴'Happy are those who mourn; God will comfort them!
⁵'Happy are those who are humble;
    they will receive what God has promised!
⁶'Happy are those whose greatest desire is to do what God requires;
    God will satisfy them fully!
⁷'Happy are those who are merciful to others;
    God will be merciful to them!
⁸'Happy are the pure in heart; they will see God!
⁹'Happy are those who work for peace;
    God will call them his children!
¹⁰'Happy are those who are persecuted because they do what God requires;
    the Kingdom of heaven belongs to them!'

Matthew 5:1-10

Television often presents images which create a desire for wealth and power. Advertisements encourage people to buy, to possess. They are out to persuade us that this is where happiness lies.
But they are wrong! To share what one has instead of hanging on to it, to give up one's place, not to claim one's turn, to strive first and foremost to bring happiness to others — that is where true happiness lies.

13

Our Father

Chapters 5, 6 and 7 of St Matthew's gospel
form a unit known as 'The Sermon on the Mount'.
It begins with the Beatitudes;
then there is a long passage in which Jesus,
commenting on the Law of Moses,
declares that he has not come to destroy it
but to bring it to perfection.
Jesus also teaches his disciples
how to pray to the Father.
He tells them about the attitude they should have
and the words they should use to address him.

On the mountain Jesus said:
6'When you pray, go to your room, close the door, and pray to your Father, who is unseen. And your Father, who sees what you do in private, will reward you.

7When you pray, do not use a lot of meaningless words, as the pagans do, who think that their gods will hear them because their prayers are long. 8Do not be like them. Your Father already knows what you need before you ask him.

9This, then, is how you should pray:

"Our Father in heaven:
May your holy name be honoured;
10   may your Kingdom come;
may your will be done on earth as it is in heaven.
11   Give us today the food we need.
12   Forgive us the wrongs we have done, as we forgive the wrongs that others have done to us.
13   Do not bring us to hard testing,
but keep us safe from the Evil One."'

Matthew 6:6-13

Jesus, the Son of God, proclaims to those who listen to him the good news that his Father is also the Father of all human beings. He teaches them that as children of the same Father they are all brothers and sisters.

It is good for us brothers and sisters to meet in the presence of the Father, and to pray to him together. To pray means to speak to God and to listen to him. Christians do this in church, when they offer up a communal prayer, but they also do it during religious instruction classes, at meetings, or at home with their families. However, that is not enough: prayer must also be, for each one of us, a personal conversation with God. That is why Jesus said: 'Pray in secret.' To pray in secret is to give God some time when one is alone with him, face to face, in peace and silence.

Jesus also tells us not to 'use a lot of meaningless words' — to repeat the same thing over and over again because we are afraid of not being understood. It is quite natural that we should tell God what we think, what is not going well for us, what we would like, just as we do with our relations and friends. But there is no point in multiplying the number of words. God loves his children, he knows them, and he is more aware than they are of what is good for them.

This then is how you should pray: 'Our Father . . .'

In the prayer which Jesus teaches his disciples, the first phrases put into words what should matter most to the children of the Father. This is that his name should be acknowledged everywhere as the name of the true God, that his kingdom of love should become a reality, that men and women everywhere should do his will.

Then it turns to us. We ask God for food (for one day only, not in order to lay in stocks and amass wealth), for his forgiveness (having made up our minds to forgive in our turn), for victory over temptation and evil.

Lord, one day your disciples said to you:
'Teach us to pray.'
I too am asking you:
teach me to pray, alone or with others,
in the words of the Our Father and in my own words,
like a true child of God.

14

Who is my neighbour?

In Palestine, and throughout the East,
to explain a teaching more clearly,
people like to tell a story,
what they call a 'parable'.
They invent characters
and imagine what happens to them,
adding numerous details
to make the account more vivid.
If the story is interesting
those listening will get a good idea
of what the storyteller wants to say.
Jesus told many parables.
Here is one of them.

[25] A teacher of the Law came up and tried to trap Jesus. 'Teacher,' he asked, 'what must I do to receive eternal life?' [26] Jesus answered him, 'What do the Scriptures say? How do you interpret them?' [27] The man answered, ' "Love the Lord your God with all your heart, with all your soul, with all your strength, and with all your mind"; and "Love your neighbour as you love yourself." ' [28] 'You are right,' Jesus replied; 'do this and you will live.' [29] But the teacher of the Law wanted to justify himself, so he asked 'Who is my neighbour?'

[30] Jesus answered, 'There was once a man who was going down from Jerusalem to Jericho when robbers attacked him, stripped him, and beat him up, leaving him half dead. [31] It so happened that a priest was going down that road; but when he saw the man, he walked on by, on the other side. [32] In the same way a Levite also came along, went over and looked at the man, and then walked on by, on the other side. [33] But a Samaritan who was travelling that way came upon the man, and when he saw him, his heart was filled with pity. [34] He went over to him, poured oil and wine on his wounds and bandaged them; then he put the man on his own animal and took him to an inn, where he took care of him . . .'

[36] And Jesus concluded, 'In your opinion, which one of these three acted like a neighbour towards the man attacked by the robbers?' [37] The teacher of the Law answered, 'The one who was kind to him.' Jesus replied, 'You go, then, and do the same.'

Luke 10:25-34 . 36-37

The desert of Juda between Jerusalem and Jericho.

*Lord Jesus,
help me to notice those around me
who wait for a word, a smile, a good turn;
help me to see people as you see them,
whether or not I like them
and to be a neighbour to them all.*

This time the man who questions Jesus in order to catch him out is a 'teacher of the Law': a professor who has studied and who teaches the Bible. 'What must I do?' he asks Jesus. To this question Jesus replies with another question: 'What do the Scriptures say? How do you interpret them?'

The man gives an excellent answer. First he quotes what is for the Jews the great commandment, a rule so important that they repeat it every day in their prayer (see volume I, chapter 5): 'Love the Lord your God with all your heart . . .' (Deuteronomy 6:5). He then adds these words, taken from another book in the Bible (Leviticus 19:18): 'Love your neighbour as yourself.'

By linking love of God and love of neighbour together like this, he has described perfectly the way of life with God. So Jesus, approving of this, congratulates the teacher of the Law. The latter, irritated, asks him another question: 'Who is my neighbour?' Jesus could have replied quite simply: your neighbour is anyone who is close to you, your family, your friends, the other teachers, your pupils and so on. But the other man is watching him intently . . . will Jesus add that tax collectors, pagans and Roman soldiers are also his neighbour?

What Jesus does is to tell the story of the Good Samaritan. He makes no comment nor does he judge the characters involved. But everyone understands well enough what the parable means. A priest and a levite (a Temple servant) pass by a wounded man without helping him, while a Samaritan who comes along shortly after looks after him. The Jews despised the Samaritans and regarded themselves as very superior to them. But in Jesus' parable it is the Samaritan who is shown to be the good and generous person who puts himself out for a stranger, knowing how to stand by him, to be his neighbour.

Jesus concludes by saying to the teacher of the Law: 'You go, then, and do the same.' Stand by anyone who needs you, Jew or Samaritan, someone you know or someone you don't know; make that person your neighbour.

15

My son was lost and has been found

In chapter 15 of St Luke's gospel, the parable of the prodigal son follows two others. The first describes a shepherd, who having lost a sheep from his flock, searches for it on the mountainside, finds it and, filled with joy, brings it back to the sheepfold. The other tells of a woman who has lost a coin. She looks all over the house for it, finds it and asks her neighbours to share in her joy. But the joy of the the father who recovers his son is far greater than either of these.

[11] Jesus went on to say, 'There was once a man who had two sons. [12] The younger one said to him, "Father, give me my share of the property now." So the man divided his property between his two sons. [13] After a few days the younger son sold his part of the property and left home with the money. He went to a country far away, where he wasted his money in reckless living. [14] He spent everything he had. Then a severe famine spread over that country, and he was left without a thing. [15] So he went to work for one of the citizens of that country, who sent him out to his farm to take care of the pigs. [16] He wished he could fill himself with the bean pods the pigs ate, but no one gave him anything to eat. [17] At last he came to his senses and said, "All my father's hired workers have more than they can eat, and here I am about to starve! [18] I will get up and go to my father and say, Father, I have sinned against God and against you. [19] I am no longer fit to be called your son; treat me as one of your hired workers." [20] So he got up and started back to his father.

'He was still a long way from home when his father saw him; his heart was filled with pity, and he ran, threw his arms round his son, and kissed him. [21] "Father," the son said, "I have sinned against God and against you. I am no longer fit to be called your son." [22] But the father called his servants. "Hurry!" he said. "Bring the best robe and put it on him. Put a ring on his finger and shoes on his feet. [23] Then go and get the prize calf and kill it, and let us celebrate with a feast! [24] For this son of mine was dead, but now he is alive; he was lost, but now he has been found." And so the feasting began.

[25] 'In the meantime the elder son was out in the field. On his way back, when he came close to the house, he heard the music and dancing. [26] So he called one of the servants and asked him, "What's going on?" [27] "Your brother has come back home," the servant answered, "and your father has killed the prize calf, because he got him back safe and sound."

[28] 'The elder brother was so angry that he would not go into the house; so his father came out and begged him to come in. [29] But he answered his father, "Look, all these years I have worked for you like a slave, and I have never disobeyed your orders. What have you given me? Not even a goat for me to have a feast with my friends! [30] But this son of yours wasted all your property on prostitutes, and when he comes back home, you kill the prize calf for him!" [31] "My son," the father answered, "you are always here with me, and everything I have is yours. [32] But we had to celebrate and be happy, because your brother was dead, but now he is alive; he was lost, but now he has been found."'

Luke 15:11-32

If you read this parable too quickly, the danger is that you will react like the elder son. The father, you will think, is not being fair. He treats his younger son better than the other, who has always remained at home to work at his father's side. However, if you read carefully, you will see that Jesus' aim was not to teach people how to deal with an ungrateful child, but to reveal something much more important: how God behaves towards his human children.

If everyone is to understand fully what 'God is love' means, it is not enough simply to repeat the words. So Jesus tells the story of a father and his sons. Through the love of the father, this parable reveals the heart of God. It recalls the words in which the prophet Hosea (see volume I, chapter 18) gave expression to the tenderness of God and God's forgiveness, which is always available, despite the evil conduct of his people.

In this parable the father is not just in the way a judge, who must apply the same law to all, is just. He is far more than just, he is 'love'.
Because he loves his son,
— he allows him his freedom . . . and therefore the opportunity to experiment and even to make stupid mistakes.
— he waits impatiently for his return.
— when he does return he throws a party, in this way showing that he still loves him, that he forgives him, and that his joy is complete.

The elder son, on the other hand, does not forgive his brother. He is angry with his brother for having gone off and frittered away the family fortune, leaving him to do all the work on the farm. He himself has always done what he should, and he would like to be rewarded for it: that, he feels, would be 'just'! And he cannot understand his father's joy because he has totally failed to understand his love.

What Jesus teaches through this story is that God does not judge his children; he loves them, always. God welcomes all who turn to him, and he invites them to join in the feast.

A joyful reunion.

When we are cut off from God, when we have grieved him through our sins, we must not hesitate to return to him and ask his pardon. It brings great joy to our Father, who is always waiting for us. In the sacrament of reconciliation he takes us in his arms and speaks to us of his love. Reconciliation is like a great feast.

16 Then Jesus took bread

The fourth gospel is that of St John.
We read one passage from it (chapter 11),
which told of the meeting between Jesus
and a woman from Samaria.
We have seen, on page 21,
how John was called by Jesus to follow him.
John was the brother of James
and the son of Zebedee the fisherman.
Jesus chose him as an apostle.
He was the youngest
and also the most enthusiastic: known as
'the disciple whom Jesus loved'.
He died at a great age — almost a hundred
— in Ephesus, in the Christian community
founded there by St Paul.
He tirelessly repeated Christ's message:
'God is love . . . Love one another . . .'
His gospel bears witness
to his experience of life with Jesus;
before he started writing
he prayed for a long time
and reflected on his memories.

[1]After this, Jesus went across Lake Galilee (or, Lake Tiberias, as it is also called). [2]A large crowd followed him, because they had seen his miracles of healing those who were ill. [3]Jesus went up a hill and sat down with his disciples. [4]The time for the Passover Festival was near. [5]Jesus looked round and saw that a large crowd was coming to him, so he asked Philip, 'Where can we buy enough food to feed all these people?' ([6]He said this to test Philip; actually he already knew what he would do.)

[7]Philip answered, 'For everyone to have even a little, it would take more than two hundred silver coins to buy enough bread.'

Multiplication of the loaves.
Wood engraving.
Commentary on the Gospels (1482).

⁸Another of his disciples, Andrew, who was Simon Peter's brother, said, ⁹'There is a boy here who has five loaves of barley bread and two fish. But they will certainly not be enough for all these people.'
¹⁰'Make the people sit down,' Jesus told them. (There was a lot of grass there.) So all the people sat down; there were about five thousand men. ¹¹Jesus took the bread, gave thanks to God, and distributed it to the people who were sitting there. He did the same with the fish, and they all had as much as they wanted. ¹²When they were all full, he said to his disciples, 'Gather the pieces left over; let us not waste any.' ¹³So they gathered them all up and filled twelve baskets with the pieces left over from the five barley loaves which the people had eaten.

¹⁴Seeing this miracle that Jesus had performed, the people there said, 'Surely this is the Prophet who was to come into the world!' ¹⁵Jesus knew that they were about to come and seize him in order to make him king by force; so he went off again to the hills by himself.

John 6:1-15

*Lord, you do not want men and women to be hungry, and you fed those who gathered round you.
Today millions of people suffer and die from hunger.
We have the scientific knowledge to end this evil, if only all would apply themselves to the problem with love and goodwill.
Lord, give us courage to do something
for the starving in the Sahel, in Brazil, in India. . . .*

Jesus performed miracles — prodigious actions — to act as signs. A sign is something visible which helps us to understand an invisible reality. On the road a green light 'signifies' permission to go; giving flowers or sending a letter 'signifies' a loving thought; the preparation of a cradle 'signifies' that a baby is expected. When Jesus cured people who were blind, paralysed or suffering from leprosy, he did so not only to bring their suffering to an end but also to show that he brought light, strength, new life. The healing of the body is a sign of another reality: that Jesus came to save us.

Jesus multiplies bread and fishes at a time when 'the Jewish Passover festival is near'. This festival is celebrated with a solemn meal. During the passover meal the Jews thank God for the bread they are eating and the wine they are drinking, but they thank him above all for the deliverance of their ancestors who were slaves in Egypt (see volume I, chapter 3). They thank God who saved his people then and who remains at their side at each moment of their history.

Jesus, by performing a miracle, feeds five thousand people, and the bread he gives foreshadows a new passover meal. But those around him only think of their bodily hunger, not of any other sort. Jesus' power impresses them and they say to one another: he must surely be God's messenger, the great prophet for whom we are waiting. They would like to see him use his power to liberate the country and get rid of its Roman occupiers. They dream of making him their king.

They never ask themselves whether Jesus' mission is to establish a kingdom on earth, or to point through his signs to another kingdom. . . . It is true that he came to satisfy the hunger of the human race. But which hunger are we in fact talking about when we say that?

17 I am the living bread

In the gospel this passage continues the narrative on the previous page: Jesus hides from the people and goes off. They want to proclaim him king, to use his power for political ends. But his mission is not political.

²²Next day when the crowd which had stayed on the other side of the lake . . . ²⁴saw that Jesus was not there, nor his disciples, they got into the boats and went to Capernaum, looking for him.

²⁵When the people found Jesus, they said to him, 'Teacher, when did you get here?'

²⁶Jesus answered, 'I am telling you the truth: you are looking for me because you ate the bread and had all you wanted, not because you understood my miracles. . . .

³⁰They replied, 'What miracle will you perform so that we may see it and believe you? What will you do? ³¹Our ancestors ate manna in the desert, just as the scripture says, "He gave them bread from heaven to eat."'

³²'I am telling you the truth,' Jesus said. 'What Moses gave you was not the bread from heaven; it is my Father who gives you the real bread from heaven. ³³For the bread that God gives is he who comes down from heaven and gives life to the world.'

³⁴'Sir,' they asked him, 'give us this bread always.' . . .

⁵¹Jesus said, 'I am the living bread that came down from heaven. If anyone eats this bread, he will live for ever. The bread that I will give him is my flesh, which I give so that the world may live.'

⁵²This started an angry argument among them. 'How can this man give us his flesh to eat?' they asked.

⁵³Jesus said to them, 'I am telling you the truth: if you do not eat the flesh of the Son of Man and drink his blood, you will not have life in yourselves. . . .

⁶⁰Many of his followers heard this and said, 'This teaching is too hard. Who can listen to it?'

⁶¹Without being told, Jesus knew that they were grumbling about this, so he said to them, 'Does this make you want to give up? . . . ⁶³What gives life is God's Spirit; man's power is of no use at all. The words I have spoken to you bring God's life-giving Spirit. ⁶⁴Yet some of you do not believe.' . . .

⁶⁶Because of this, many of Jesus' followers turned back and would not go with him any more. ⁶⁷So he asked the twelve disciples, 'And you — would you also like to leave?'

⁶⁸Simon Peter answered him, 'Lord, to whom would we go? You have the words that give eternal life. ⁶⁹And now we believe. . . .'

John 6

For Christians, the bread of life is the body of Jesus offered in the Eucharist. This is recalled in the words said as we are offered the host: 'The body of Christ', to which we reply: 'Amen'. In so doing we express our faith, our assent. It is as though we were saying to Jesus: 'We believe that you are present. You have the words of eternal life.'

The crowd ate their fill of loaves and fishes. But they failed to understand that this food was a sign revealing the nature of Jesus' mission. They wanted to have this man who could perform such wonders for their benefit as their king. They remember that Moses fed their ancestors in the desert: they had nothing to do but gather the manna each morning (see volume I, chapter 4). That is why they search for Jesus and eventually catch up with him in Capernaum. He tells them, however, that the manna was not the true bread from heaven. God is giving them this true bread now.

What then, is this bread that gives true life, life which lasts forever, the very life of God? It is Jesus himself. His listeners do not understand. They cannot understand. How can this man Jesus give his body as food? Are we going to have to eat him? That would be unthinkable.

The people protest: he is mad! We cannot go on listening to him. Jesus, however, does not take back what he has said . . . rather he insists: 'If you do not eat the flesh of the Son of Man and drink his blood, you will not have life.' And he adds: 'What gives life is God's Spirit,' for Jesus has come to communicate to all human beings the spirit and life of God. It is their hunger for God that he wants to satisfy. But they do not realise this. So many of them go off, so that they do not have to listen to any more of his preaching, which they find shocking.

Only the apostles remain with Jesus. It may be that they have understood no better than the others, but they trust him. For them, his words are true. 'Lord,' says Peter, speaking for them all, 'to whom would we go? You have the words of eternal life.' What Jesus' words actually mean will become clearer to them later on.

18

Who do you say I am?

Caesarea,
a new town
built in honour
of the Emperor Augustus,
is situated
in northern Galilee,
near the countries
where the pagans lived.
Jesus goes there
with his apostles
to get away from
the crowds.
While they are there,
he asks the apostles:
what have they heard
people say about him
in the villages
they have visited?
The disciples repeat
some rather bizarre
statements
which nevertheless show
that Jesus is regarded
as a man of God,
a prophet.
Jesus interrupts them
to ask:
'What about you?
Who do you say I am?'
For that
is the essential question.

[13] Jesus went to the territory near the town of Caesarea Philippi, where he asked his disciples, 'Who do people say the Son of Man is?'

[14] 'Some say John the Baptist,' they answered. 'Others say Elijah, while others say Jeremiah or some other prophet.'

[15] 'What about you?' he asked. 'Who do you say I am?'

[16] Simon Peter answered, 'You are the Messiah, the Son of the living God.'

[17] 'Good for you, Simon son of John!' answered Jesus. 'For this truth did not come to you from any human being, but it was given to you directly by my Father in heaven. [18] And so I tell you, Peter: you are a rock, and on this rock foundation I will build my church, and not even death will ever be able to overcome it. [19] I will give you the keys of the Kingdom of heaven; what you prohibit on earth will be prohibited in heaven, and what you permit on earth will be permitted in heaven.'

[20] Then Jesus ordered his disciples not to tell anyone that he was the Messiah.

[21] From that time on Jesus began to say plainly to his disciples, 'I must go to Jerusalem and suffer much from the elders, the chief priests, and the teachers of the Law. I will be put to death, but three days later I will be raised to life.'

Matthew 16:13-21

The disciples are continually in Jesus' company, they listen to him, they follow him. They get to know him better and better and believe that he is speaking for God. But now, for the first time, one of their number, Simon, is able to say: 'You are the Christ (Messiah), the Son of the living God.' Jesus answers him: you are fortunate to have that faith within you, because it is not your human intelligence that has enabled you to see that; only my Father could have revealed to you who I am. God alone can grant it to someone to know who Jesus is and to believe in him.

Simon said who he believed Jesus to be. In return Jesus said to Simon: 'I tell you Peter: you are a rock, and on this rock foundation I will build my Church.' Jesus changes Simon's name because in charging him with a new mission, he has made a new man of him. For Jesus, Simon is the stone, the rock, the rock foundation on which he is going to build his Church, the community of believers. It will have as its foundation Simon Peter's faith in Jesus the Christ, the Son of God.

The Church is the community of those who share this faith in Jesus Christ. Jesus announced it on this day and he promised that it would survive all dangers and triumph over the forces of evil. The Church will carry on for all time Jesus' work on earth. With minds enlightened by the Father, the apostles now know that Jesus is the Messiah, but the strange thing is that they are to keep it secret. This is because they still have to learn what the true mission of the Messiah is: that is, to found not an earthly kingdom but the kingdom of God. They have also got to accept Christ's passage through death, on the cross, and his resurrection. After that they will be able to proclaim their faith. But they still have a long way to go!

St Peter. Thirteenth century mosaic.
Basilica of St Mark. Venice.

Who is Jesus for you?
How would you reply if your friends at school asked you this question?

19 Do not be afraid

At Caesarea
Simon Peter expressed his faith in Jesus:
'You are the Messiah,
the Son of the living God!'
But, to prevent his disciples from thinking
he would be a powerful and victorious king,
Jesus warned them he would be persecuted
and put to death.
He also told them he would rise again.
But what did that mean?
The apostles did not understand
and were worried.
Six days later
Jesus gave three of them a glimpse
of what his resurrection would be like.

¹Six days later Jesus took with him Peter and the brothers James and John and led them up a high mountain where they were alone. ²As they looked on, a change came over Jesus: his face was shining like the sun, and his clothes were dazzling white. ³Then the three disciples saw Moses and Elijah talking with Jesus. ⁴So Peter spoke up and said to Jesus, 'Lord, how good it is that we are here! If you wish, I will make three tents here, one for you, one for Moses, and one for Elijah.'

⁵While he was talking, a shining cloud came over them, and a voice from the cloud said, 'This is my own dear Son, with whom I am pleased — listen to him!'

⁶When the disciples heard the voice, they were so terrified that they threw themselves face downwards on the ground. ⁷Jesus came to them and touched them. 'Get up,' he said. 'Don't be afraid!' ⁸So they looked up and saw no one there but Jesus.

⁹As they came down the mountain, Jesus ordered them, 'Don't tell anyone about this vision you have seen until the Son of Man has been raised from death.'

Matthew 17:1-9

Once again an important event takes place on a mountain (probably Mount Thabor in Galilee). A mountain is a place of solitude, silence and prayer. It is therefore a good place for meeting with God. The Bible draws attention to this, particularly in the case of Moses and Elijah.

Moses handed down the Law and solemnised the covenant between God and the people of Israel. The great prophet Elijah was, throughout his life, a fearless spokesman for God. Both encountered God at the top of a mountain. And now these two prophets, who centuries earlier prepared for the coming of the Messiah, appear beside Jesus, talking to him.

As for Jesus himself, to the apostles he looks quite different from usual: he is 'transfigured'. Just as 'transpierce' means to pierce right through to the other side of something, so 'transfigure' means to go beyond the outward appearance to reach an aspect that is not usually visible. A light seems to abide within Jesus and to shine out from his person. The light of God, reflected in him, transforms him, making his whole person radiant. The life of God takes possession of his body and transfigures it, as it will transfigure it in the resurrection.

The luminous cloud indicates the presence of God. God manifests himself, just as he did at Jesus' baptism, to proclaim that Jesus is his Son and shares his life.

'Do not be afraid,' Jesus tells his friends. Do not be afraid of God: if he is present here it is to express his love. Do not be afraid, either, of my approaching death, for it will enable me to become what you have just seen: a transfigured human being.

Some paintings, icons for example, 'transfigure' the faces of Jesus, the Virgin Mary and the saints. This is to show that God dwells within them and shines forth from them. Such images help us to contemplate the light of God.

20

I must stay in your house today

The town of Jericho is not in Galilee. It is situated near the point where the Jordan flows into the Dead Sea. On his way to Jerusalem, Jesus passes through Jericho. He has never lived here but the people have heard of him. A great crowd gathers as he goes through.

¹Jesus went on into Jericho and was passing through. ²There was a chief tax collector there named Zacchaeus, who was rich. ³He was trying to see who Jesus was, but he was a little man and could not see Jesus because of the crowd. ⁴So he ran ahead of the crowd and climbed a sycamore tree to see Jesus, who was going to pass that way. ⁵When Jesus came to that place, he looked up and said to Zacchaeus, 'Hurry down, Zacchaeus, because I must stay in your house today.'

⁶Zacchaeus hurried down and welcomed him with great joy. ⁷All the people who saw it started grumbling. 'This man has gone as a guest to the home of a sinner!'

⁸Zacchaeus stood up and said to the Lord, 'Listen, sir! I will give half my belongings to the poor, and if I have cheated anyone, I will pay him back four times as much.'

⁹Jesus said to him, 'Salvation has come to this house today, for this man, also, is a descendant of Abraham. ¹⁰The Son of Man came to seek and to save the lost.'

Luke 19:1-10

Over the heads of the people surrounding him, Jesus catches sight of Zacchaeus and decides to go to his house. It is an astonishing choice. Zacchaeus is the chief tax collector. He has made a fortune stealing from his fellow townspeople, who fear and despise him. Yet here is Jesus telling him in front of everyone: 'I must stay in your house today.'

Jesus says 'I must', not 'I want to'. It is part of his mission: he who has come 'to seek and save the lost' has gone in preference towards sinners. Just as Jesus called the tax collector Matthew to be his disciple, so he calls on Zacchaeus to welcome him into his home.

Jesus looked at Zacchaeus and spoke to him; his words seemed so simple, but they were full of meaning. Zacchaeus wanted to see Jesus; he asked nothing of him. Then Jesus calls him by name and invites himself to Zacchaeus' house for a meal. It is as though he were saying: I know who you are and what you have done, but I am coming to prove to you that God still loves you.

The friendship Jesus shows him surprises Zacchaeus — fills him with joy and instantaneously works a change of heart within him. He becomes aware of all the wrong he has done and decides to change his life: he is going to give half his fortune to the poor and pay back fourfold those he has cheated.

Zacchaeus is set free from his sin, from his attachment to money. He will experience life in a new way. With Jesus, 'God who saves', freedom and joy have entered his house. And Jesus declares: Zacchaeus is saved because he is a son of Abraham, thanks, that is, to the promises made by God to Abraham and his descendants (see volume I, chapter 12). Zacchaeus has not deserved his pardon, his salvation. God has given them to him out of love.

Zacchaeus.
Wood engraving.
Commentary on the Gospels (1482).

The way Jesus looked at him transformed Zacchaeus
and filled him with a desire to live life differently.
Had Jesus looked at him with contempt,
as a thief incapable of changing his ways,
Zacchaeus would have remained as he was and continued to steal.

Lord, help me to look at others with love and trust,
never rejecting or condemning them.

21 I am the resurrection and the life

Bethany is a village
in the countryside near Jerusalem,
on the way to Jericho.
In this village lived a man called Lazarus,
with his two sisters, Martha and Mary.
Jesus loved them very much,
and he often stayed with them
when he came to Jerusalem.
One day Lazarus fell seriously ill.
His sisters sent a message telling Jesus.
But when he arrived in Bethany
Lazarus was already dead.

[17] When Jesus arrived, he found that Lazarus had been buried four days before. [18] Bethany was less than three kilometres from Jerusalem, [19] and many Judaeans had come to see Martha and Mary to comfort them over their brother's death.

[20] When Martha heard that Jesus was coming, she went out to meet him, but Mary stayed in the house. [21] Martha said to Jesus, 'If you had been here, Lord, my brother would not have died! [22] But I know that even now God will give you whatever you ask him for.'

[23] 'Your brother will rise to life,' Jesus told her.

[24] 'I know,' she replied, 'that he will rise to life on the last day.'

[25] Jesus said to her, 'I am the resurrection and the life. Whoever believes in me will live, even though he dies; [26] and whoever lives and believes in me will never die. Do you believe this?' [27] 'Yes, Lord!' she answered. 'I do believe that you are the Messiah, the Son of God, who was to come into the world.'

[28] After Martha said this, she went back and called her sister Mary privately. 'The Teacher is here,' she told her, 'and is asking for you.' [29] When Mary heard this, she got up and hurried out to meet him. ([30] Jesus had not yet arrived in the village, but was still in the place where Martha had met him.) [31] The people who were in the house with Mary, comforting her, followed her when they saw her get up and hurry out. They thought that she was going to the grave to weep there.

[32] Mary arrived where Jesus was, and as soon as she saw

Resurrection of Lazarus. Thirteenth century. Church of Saint-Denis at Pontigné (France).

him, she fell at his feet. 'Lord,' she said, 'if you had been here, my brother would not have died!'

³³Jesus saw her weeping, and he saw how the people who were with her were weeping also; his heart was touched, and he was deeply moved. ³⁴'Where have you buried him?' he asked them.

'Come and see, Lord,' they answered. ³⁵Jesus wept. ³⁶'See how much he loved him!' the people said.

³⁷But some of them said, 'He gave sight to the blind man, didn't he? Could he not have kept Lazarus from dying?'

³⁸Deeply moved once more, Jesus went to the tomb, which was a cave with a stone placed at the entrance. ³⁹'Take the stone away!' Jesus ordered.

Martha, the dead man's sister, answered, 'There will be a bad smell, Lord. He has been buried four days!'

⁴⁰Jesus said to her, 'Didn't I tell you that you would see God's glory if you believed?' ⁴¹They took the stone away. Jesus looked up and said, 'I thank you, Father, that you listen to me. ⁴²I know that you always listen to me, but I say this for the sake of the people here, so that they will believe that you sent me.' ⁴³After he had said this, he called out in a loud voice, 'Lazarus, come out!' ⁴⁴He came out, his hands and feet wrapped in grave clothes, and with a cloth round his face. 'Untie him,' Jesus told them, 'and let him go.'

⁴⁵Many of the people who had come to visit Mary saw what Jesus did, and they believed in him.

John 11:17-45

To learn of the death of someone one loves and to know that one will never see that person again is a very saddening experience. It is impossible not to be deeply distressed by it. Beside the grave of his friend Lazarus, Jesus weeps.

When they see him, some of the people say to one another: 'He gave sight to the blind man, didn't he? Could he not have kept Lazarus from dying?' Well, certainly he could have done — he had cured other sick people. But Jesus did not come to eliminate sickness, suffering and death. He came to live as a human being among other human beings: he wept, he suffered, he died. Then his resurrection showed that death is not the end of life but the beginning of a new and much more beautiful life.

Jesus brings Lazarus back to life. He makes him live again as he had lived before — live, that is, like everyone else, in the knowledge that one day he will die again.

This is not a resurrection. To rise again is not to return to life in the sense of going back to something that is already behind one; it is to pass on to another life, in the way a caterpillar becomes a butterfly. By showing himself transfigured to Peter, James and John, Jesus showed them what he would be like when he rose again.

In bringing Lazarus back from the grave, as one would wake someone from sleep, Jesus is asserting that he is the master of death and can triumph over it. The multiplication of the loaves was a foreshadowing, a promise, a sign of the Eucharist. In the same way, by bringing Lazarus back to life, Jesus announces and offers a sign of the resurrection promised to us all.

He can truly say: 'I am the resurrection and the life.'

When those we love die, we weep. And we are sometimes tempted to think that they have died forever; that we have lost them for good.
But because we trust Jesus, we believe, like Martha, that his words and promises are true. Even if we do not understand how it will come about, we believe that we will all rise again after him and like him. We believe that after death we will see all those we love again and be happy with them in the presence of God.

22

You did it for me

In Jerusalem, during the days
before his arrest and death,
Jesus often talked to his disciples
about the future.
He promised them that when the time came
for the world to end,
he would return as king of the universe.
Like Jesus the world as we know it will die
and like Jesus, it will be transformed.
The long struggle between good and evil
will be over
and the kingdom of God
will be established forever.

³¹'When the Son of Man comes as King and all the angels with him, he will sit on his royal throne, ³²and the people of all the nations will be gathered before him. Then he will divide them into two groups, just as a shepherd separates the sheep from the goats. ³³He will put the righteous people on his right and the others on his left. ³⁴Then the King will say to the people on his right, "Come, you that are blessed by my Father! Come and possess the kingdom which has been prepared for you ever since the creation of the world. ³⁵I was hungry and you fed me, thirsty and you gave me a drink; I was a stranger and you received me in your homes, ³⁶naked and you clothed me; I was sick and you took care of me, in prison and you visited me."

³⁷'The righteous will then answer him, "When, Lord, did we ever see you hungry and feed you, or thirsty and give you a drink? ³⁸When did we ever see you a stranger and welcome you in our homes, or naked and clothe you? ³⁹When did we ever see you sick or in prison, and visit you?" ⁴⁰The King will reply, "I tell you, whenever you did

this for one of the least important of these brothers of mine, you did it for me!"

⁴¹"Then he will say to those on his left, "Away from me, you that are under God's curse! Away to the eternal fire which has been prepared for the Devil and his angels! ⁴²I was hungry but you would not feed me, thirsty but you would not give me a drink; ⁴³I was a stranger but you would not welcome me in your homes, naked but you would not clothe me; I was sick and in prison but you would not take care of me."

⁴⁴'Then they will answer him, "When Lord, did we ever see you hungry or thirsty or a stranger or naked or sick or in prison, and would not help you?" ⁴⁵The King will reply, "I tell you, whenever you refused to help one of these least important ones, you refused to help me." ⁴⁶These, then, will be sent off to eternal punishment, but the righteous will go to eternal life.'

Matthew 25:31-46

The Last Judgment. Thirteenth century manuscript. Psalter. Bibliothèque Sainte-Geneviève. Paris.

Are you aware, at school, or in your street or block of flats, or in your area, of children who are made unwelcome because they are strangers? of elderly people who are alone? of people who are sick or hungry? Reread this passage from the gospel and ask yourself what you can do for them.

To emphasise the fact that he really is a human being, Jesus is often referred to as the 'Son of Man'. The name becomes even more striking once he is revealed as a king, coming from heaven to judge all men and women with the power of God. Talking about the end of the world, Jesus describes a vast gathering at which he himself separates the good from the wicked. By speaking in terms of sheep and goats, he also reminds us that he is a shepherd, one who watches over his flock. Jesus is indeed the just king, the 'prince of peace' announced by the prophets: the Messiah.

Yet, reading this passage from the gospel, it is possible to think that Jesus is a severe judge, who sends off those who have not obeyed his commandments to burn forever. That, however, is only an image: there is no actual fire into which the wicked are thrown. Jesus merely uses the images that were habitually used at that time, to make himself understood. What he wants to make clear is that we will be happy after death if we have loved our fellow human beings. Those who love during their life on earth will continue to live in love, happy forever in the kingdom of God. And those who live without loving will remain forever far from God.

Thus Jesus comes back continually to the same commandment: 'Love one another.' He emphasises that to love is not simply to wish one's neighbour well. It means expressing love for that person through one's actions — it means giving him or her food and clothing, welcoming strangers, visiting the sick and even those in prison. Love means paying attention to other people, noticing what they need, sharing with them one's money and one's time (see page 36, the story of the good Samaritan).

But that is not all! To love one's neighbour is to love Jesus. That is the really astonishing thing. When he declares: 'You did it for me,' Jesus is saying: the poor person wanting to be loved and helped is myself! And so, whenever we give food, clothing or time to those who are strangers to us, to the sick, the hungry or the imprisoned, we are feeding, clothing and visiting Jesus.

Jesus, who became a human being among the poor, declares that he will be present until the end of the world in those who have least.

The Passover of Jesus

23 Take it,

For nearly three years,
through what he did and what he said,
Jesus made known his Father's love for mankind.
Several times he told his disciples
that sometime soon
he would be prevented from speaking,
arrested, condemned and put to death.
It is by dying that he will at last
reveal the love of God in its fullness.
Jesus' arrest, his trial, his execution,
his being laid in the tomb
and the discovery of his resurrection
will take place over four days,
from Thursday to Sunday.
All four evangelists record these events,
each in his own way
(we are going to read Mark's account).
However, all make clear that the Passion
(the period of Christ's suffering)
and the Resurrection are the 'Passover' of Jesus.
The word 'passover' means 'passage'.
For the Jews, the great Passover feast,
which is celebrated every year,
recalls the 'passover' experienced
by their ancestors under Moses:
the passage from a land where they were slaves
to a land where they were free.
Jesus, for his part,
passes 'from this world to the Father',
as St John puts it;
he leaves this life and passes through death
in order to be reborn to a new life.

One of the first representations of the Last Supper. Catacomb of St Calixtus. Rome.

this is my body

¹²On the first day of the Festival of Unleavened Bread, ... ²²while they were eating, Jesus took a piece of bread, gave a prayer of thanks, broke it, and gave it to his disciples. 'Take it,' he said, 'this is my body.'

²³Then he took a cup, gave thanks to God, and handed it to them; and they all drank from it. ²⁴Jesus said, 'This is my blood which is poured out for many, my blood which seals God's covenant.' ...

²⁶Then they sang a hymn and went out to the Mount of Olives. ...

³²They came to a place called Gethsemane, and Jesus said to his disciples, 'Sit here while I pray.' ³³He took Peter, James, and John with him. Distress and anguish came over him, ³⁴and he said to them, 'The sorrow in my heart is so great that it almost crushes me. Stay here and keep watch.' ³⁵He went a little farther on, threw himself on the ground, and prayed that, if possible, he might not have to go through that time of suffering. ³⁶'Father,' he prayed, 'my Father! All things are possible for you. Take this cup of suffering away from me. Yet not what I want, but what you want.'

³⁷Then he returned and found the three disciples asleep. He said to Peter, 'Simon, are you asleep? Weren't you able to stay awake even for one hour?' ³⁸And he said to them, 'Keep watch, and pray that you will not fall into temptation.' ...

⁴³Jesus was still speaking when Judas, one of the twelve disciples, arrived. With him was a crowd armed with swords and clubs, and sent by the chief priests, the teachers of the Law, and the elders. ⁴⁴The traitor had given the crowd a signal: 'The man I kiss is the one you want. Arrest him and take him away under guard.'

⁴⁵As soon as Judas arrived, he went up to Jesus and said, 'Teacher!' and kissed him. ⁴⁶So they arrested Jesus and held him tight. ...

⁵⁰Then all the disciples left him and ran away.

Mark 14

It is Thursday . . . the day known to Christians as 'Maundy Thursday'. Sometime before Jesus had said: 'No one takes my life away from me. I give it up of my own free will.'

He gives it when he offers himself as food, as he said he would (chapter 17). In the course of the passover meal, which he celebrates according to the custom of his people, Jesus tells his apostles: 'Take it, this is my body. . . . This is my blood which is poured out for many, my blood which seals God's covenant.' According to Luke and Paul he added: 'Do this in memory of me' (chapter 36). In this way Jesus invites all men and women to enter into a new covenant with God; and at the same time he asks them to reenact this covenant meal after he has gone, in order to acknowledge him in their midst and receive his life.

Jesus gives his life, fully accepting in advance what awaits him. He could run away, leave Jerusalem. He does not do so. As he has so often done before, he retires to the garden of Gethsemane, but this time it is not to rest. As Jesus goes towards suffering and death, his human heart is seized with panic and he prays to be spared. Yet he tells the Father immediately: 'Not what I want but what you want.' The Father's will is obviously not that he should suffer, but that he should be faithful to his mission and go on loving until the end. 'For the greatest love a person can have for his friends is to give his life for them.'

The apostles chosen by Jesus have not managed to stay awake to give him support and pray with him. Not even Peter, James and John, the three witnesses of his transfiguration (chapter 19), the three who are closest to him! Jesus asks them to stay with him and they go to sleep. He is alone in his anguish, alone in his prayer. And when he is taken prisoner, his friends, instead of defending him, flee.

55

24 He deserves to die

⁵³Then Jesus was taken to the High Priest's house. . . . ⁶⁰The High Priest stood up in front of them all and questioned Jesus, . . . ⁶¹'Are you the Messiah, the Son of the Blessed God?' ⁶²'I am,' answered Jesus, 'and you will all see the Son of Man seated on the right of the Almighty and coming with the clouds of heaven!' ⁶³The High Priest tore his robes and said, 'We don't need any more witnesses! ⁶⁴You heard his blasphemy. What is your decision?' They all voted against him: he was guilty and should be put to death. . . .

⁶⁶Peter was still down in the courtyard when one of the High Priest's servant-girls came by. ⁶⁷When she saw Peter warming himself, she looked straight at him and said, 'You, too, were with Jesus of Nazareth.' ⁶⁸But he denied it. 'I don't know. . . . I don't understand what you are talking about,' he answered, and went out into the passage. Just then a cock crowed. ⁶⁹The servant-girl saw him there and began to repeat to the bystanders, 'He is one of them!' ⁷⁰But Peter denied it again. A little while later the bystanders accused Peter again. 'You can't deny that you are one of them, because you, too, are from Galilee.' ⁷¹Then Peter said, 'I swear that I am telling the truth! May God punish me if I am not! I do not know the man you are talking about!' ⁷²Just then a cock crowed a second time, and Peter remembered how Jesus had said to him, 'Before the cock crows twice, you will say three times that you do not know me.' And he broke down and cried.

15 Early in the morning the chief priests met hurriedly with the elders, the teachers of the Law, and the whole Council, and made their plans. They put Jesus in chains, led him away, and handed him over to Pilate. ²Pilate questioned him, 'Are you the king of the Jews?' Jesus answered, 'So you say.' ³The chief priests were accusing Jesus of many things, ⁴so Pilate questioned him again, 'Aren't you going to answer? Listen to all their accusations!' ⁵Again Jesus refused to say a word, and Pilate was amazed.

Jesus presented to the Jews by Pilate.
Fifteenth century fresco. Church at Brigue (France).

⁶At every Passover Festival Pilate was in the habit of setting free any one prisoner the people asked for. ⁷At that time a man named Barabbas was in prison with the rebels who had committed murder in the riot. ⁸When the crowd gathered and began to ask Pilate for the usual favour, ⁹he asked them, 'Do you want me to set free for you the king of the Jews?' ¹⁰He knew very well that the chief priests had handed Jesus over to him because they were jealous. ¹¹But the chief priests stirred up the crowd to ask, instead, for Pilate to set Barabbas free for them. ¹²Pilate spoke again to the crowd, 'What, then, do you want me to do with the one you call the king of the Jews?' ¹³They shouted back, 'Crucify him!' ¹⁴'But what crime has he committed?' Pilate asked. They shouted all the louder, 'Crucify him!'

¹⁵Pilate wanted to please the crowd, so he set Barabbas free for them. Then he had Jesus whipped and handed him over to be crucified.

Mark 14 and 15

From the very beginning Jesus' words and actions disturbed the priests and the pharisees. Very soon they began to hate him. They found him dangerous because he questioned their religious traditions. At all costs they wanted to get rid of him (see previous page, Mark 14:1).

After his arrest, Jesus is led before the Council of the Jews, known as the Sanhedrin. The leader of the Sanhedrin, the High Priest, asks him: 'Are you the Messiah, Son of the Blessed God?' Jesus replies that he is, adding that he will soon be in the presence of God as God's equal. For those who believe in a unique God, to claim equality with him is blasphemy. Even if the rulers of the people had not already decided to destroy him, this claim would be enough to condemn him: he deserves to die.

But in occupied Palestine, only the Romans have the right to sentence someone to death. So the High Priest and his colleagues lead Jesus before the Roman governor, Pontius Pilate. They present Jesus to him as an agitator who claims to be 'king of the Jews', and therefore a threat to Roman authority. Pilate asks him: 'Are you the king of the Jews?' to which Jesus replies simply: 'So you say.' But what sort of king? Pilate realises that the accusations brought by the Jews are false: Jesus was not trying to stir up a rebellion against the Romans.

Pilate wants to resolve the situation without creating difficulties for himself. As he is going to release one prisoner anyway on the occasion of the Jewish Passover, he proposes that he should release Jesus. But the priests incite the crowd to call for the release of Barabbas, a murderer.

Pilate gives in to them out of cowardice: he frees Barabbas and sends Jesus to his death. No one has come to Jesus' defence. Those he cured are not around. The crowd has turned against him. The apostle Peter, the friend who had promised never to abandon him, denies him three times while the sentence is being passed.

Alone in the face of lies and cowardice, Jesus, who is truly the Son of God, is going to die for this truth, and this he accepts.

[25] He who was crucified is risen!

²²They took Jesus to a place called Golgotha, which means 'The Place of the Skull.' ²³There they tried to give him wine mixed with a drug called myrrh, but Jesus would not drink it. ²⁴Then they crucified him and divided his clothes among themselves, throwing dice to see who would get which piece of clothing. ²⁵It was nine o'clock in the morning when they crucified him. ²⁶The notice of the accusation against him said: 'The King of the Jews.' . . .

³³At noon the whole country was covered with darkness, which lasted for three hours. ³⁴At three o'clock Jesus cried out with a loud shout, *'Eloi, Eloi, lema sabachthani?'* which means, 'My God, my God, why did you abandon me?' . . . ³⁷With a loud cry Jesus died.

³⁸The curtain hanging in the Temple was torn in two, from top to bottom. ³⁹The army officer who was standing there in front of the cross saw how Jesus had died. 'This man was really the Son of God!' he said. . . .

⁴²⁻⁴³It was towards evening when Joseph of Arimathea arrived. He was a respected member of the Council. . . . It was Preparation day (that is, the day before the Sabbath), so Joseph went boldly into the presence of Pilate and asked him for the body of Jesus. . . . ⁴⁵Pilate told Joseph he could have the body. ⁴⁶Joseph bought a linen sheet, took the body down, wrapped it in the sheet, and placed it in a tomb which had been dug out of solid rock. Then he rolled a large stone across the entrance to the tomb. ⁴⁷Mary Magdalene and Mary the mother of Joseph were watching and saw where the body of Jesus was placed.

16 After the Sabbath was over, Mary Magdalene, Mary the mother of James, and Salome bought spices to go and anoint the body of Jesus. ²Very early on Sunday morning, at sunrise, they went to the tomb. ³⁻⁴On the way they said to one another, 'Who will roll away the stone for us from the entrance to the tomb?' . . . Then they looked up and saw that the stone had already been rolled back. ⁵So they entered the tomb, where they saw a young man sitting on the right, wearing a white robe — and they were alarmed.

⁶'Don't be alarmed,' he said. 'I know you are looking for Jesus of Nazareth, who was crucified. He is not here — he has been raised! Look, here is the place where they put him. ⁷Now go and give this message to his disciples, including Peter: "He is going to Galilee ahead of you; there you will see him, just as he told you."'

Mark 15 and 16

The soldiers lead Jesus out of the town and nail him to the cross. He refuses the drink that would ease his suffering a little. He is abandoned by all but his mother and a few women. Alone like this, he is going to die. Then in a loud voice he begins to recite psalm 22: 'My God, my God, why have you abandoned me?' The psalm is the lament of a man tortured by his enemies. They mock him, they pierce his hands and feet, they share his clothes among themselves. From the depths of his distress he cries to the Lord, and the Lord hears him. Then he gives him thanks . . . Jesus often recited this prayer in the company of his people. On this Good Friday it expresses all he is going through.

At three o'clock Jesus utters a great cry and dies. The veil of the Temple — the curtain which prevented the people from entering the sanctuary — is torn from top to bottom. Having seen Jesus die, the centurion, the Roman officer standing beside the cross, exclaims: 'This man really was the Son of God.'

On Saturday nothing happens, because the Sabbath rest is sacrosanct.

On Sunday morning, Jesus' friends come to the tomb in which his body was hurriedly placed before the beginning of the Sabbath. Jesus' body is no longer there. But a mysterious messenger repeats Christ's own words to tell them: he is risen, he is waiting for you in Galilee. In Galilee, where the great adventure began a few years before.

'This man was the Son of God.' These words, spoken by a pagan, throw light on the whole passover of Jesus, his death and his resurrection.

Jesus was truly human. Like all human beings he suffered and he died. A victim of hatred, injustice and cowardice, he died. His body was put in a tomb.

But Jesus is also truly the Son of God. And God, who is life itself, did not allow his son to disappear without trace in his death. Jesus the man and the Son of God is still living. Rising from the dead he passed from this earthly existence to life with the Father. By his resurrection he revealed that for every human being death is not an ending but the way into the Father's presence, the beginning of a new life.

The empty tomb.
Thirteenth century bas-relief.
Church at Bourget (France).

With all Christians,
we proclaim our faith in Christ's passover.

I believe
in Jesus Christ the only Son of God,
who was born of the virgin Mary,
suffered under Pontius Pilate,
was crucified, died and was buried.
The third day he rose again from the dead,
he ascended into heaven
and is seated on the Father's right hand
and thence he shall come to judge the living and the dead.

26 Then their eyes were opened

After his resurrection,
Jesus showed himself to his disciples.
He helped them to understand
that he was alive and still with them.
The evangelists' accounts
of Jesus' appearances
differ in length and detail;
but they all have one feature in common.
The men and women Jesus approaches
do not realise immediately
that it is Jesus . . .
they hesitate . . .
sometimes they are even afraid . . .
their eyes must be opened
if they are to recognise him.

[13] On that same day two of Jesus' followers were going to a village named Emmaus, about eleven kilometres from Jerusalem, [14] and they were talking to each other about all the things that had happened. [15] As they talked and discussed, Jesus himself drew near and walked along with them; [16] they saw him, but somehow did not recognize him. [17] Jesus said to them, 'What are you talking about to each other, as you walk along?'

They stood still, with sad faces. [18] One of them, named Cleopas, asked him, 'Are you the only visitor in Jerusalem who doesn't know the things that have been happening there these last few days?'

[19] 'What things?' he asked.

'The things that happened to Jesus of Nazareth,' they answered. 'This man was a prophet and was considered by God and by all the people to be powerful in everything he said and did. [20] Our chief priests and rulers handed him over to be sentenced to death, and he was crucified. [21] And we had hoped that he would be the one who was going to set Israel free! Besides all that, this is now the third day since it happened. [22] Some of the women of our group surprised us; they went at dawn to the tomb, [23] but could not find his body. They came back saying they had seen a vision of angels who told them that he is alive. [24] Some of our group went to the tomb and found it exactly as the women had said, but they did not see him.'

[25] Then Jesus said to them, 'How foolish you are, how slow you are to believe everything the prophets said! [26] Was it not necessary for the Messiah to suffer these things and then to enter his glory?' [27] And Jesus explained to them what was said about himself in all the Scriptures, beginning with the books of Moses and the writings of all the prophets.

[28] As they came near the village to which they were going, Jesus acted as if he were going farther; [29] but they held him back, saying, 'Stay with us; the day is almost over and it is getting dark.' So he went in to stay with them. [30] He sat down to eat with them, took the bread, and said the blessing; then he broke the bread and gave it to

The disciples at Emmaus.
Thirteenth century
bas-relief.
Church at Bourget
(France).

them. ³¹Then their eyes were opened and they recognized him, but he disappeared from their sight. ³²They said to each other, 'Wasn't it like a fire burning in us when he talked to us on the road and explained the Scriptures to us?'

³³They got up at once and went back to Jerusalem, where they found the eleven disciples gathered together with the others ³⁴and saying. 'The Lord is risen indeed! He has appeared to Simon!'

³⁵The two then explained to them what had happened on the road, and how they had recognized the Lord when he broke the bread.

Luke 24:13-35

*Today we cannot meet Jesus
in the way people met him when he was on earth.
But like the first Christians and those since,
we can encounter the Lord in his word
and in the sacrament of the Eucharist.
As Jesus accompanied the disciples going to Emmaus
so he accompanies and speaks to us (in the gospel);
like them we can receive the sign of his presence (in the Eucharist).*

Jesus went through his passover — the journey which, passing through death, took him from his human life to life transfigured by his resurrection. All those who knew him as a man, as a companion, as a master, must now go through their own 'passover' in order to recognize him as the Risen One, the Lord. When Jesus approaches them their human eyes do not see that it is he. Then he gives them signs and teaches them to look with the eyes of faith.

The two disciples who have left Jerusalem are sadly making their way home. They are distressed because Jesus is dead, and they are disappointed because he has not driven the Romans out and established the Kingdom of Israel. The fact that the tomb was found empty does not appear to them to be very important, since no one has seen Jesus. The last three days have completely demoralized them and they have lost all hope.

The two disciples gladly welcome the man who comes to walk in their company, and they give him their own account of what has happened. He for his part refers to those texts in 'the scriptures' — that is the Bible — which foretell these events and tries to help them understand.

So they see Jesus and hear his teaching, yet still they do not recognize him. But soon everything becomes clear. At the table, the stranger blesses bread and gives it to them; 'then their eyes are opened'. They realise at last that this is Jesus, alive, risen, present with them. He disappears immediately, but that is not important, for they no longer have doubts. Faith has come alive within them and changed the way they look at things. They are now able to see beyond appearances and recognize the Lord.

Having had such an encounter, the two disciples cannot keep it to themselves! They leave immediately. They hurry back to Jerusalem to share with the apostles the good news they have just received: that the Lord is alive. Meanwhile, Simon Peter and his companions have also seen Jesus and believed in his resurrection.

27 Stop your doubting and believe

In the morning
of what is the first day of the week for Jews,
Jesus' women friends found his tomb empty.
At Emmaus two disciples met him,
alive and risen.
And now, that same evening
he appears to his assembled disciples.
It is Easter Day,
the day of Christ's resurrection,
the greatest event of all history.
This day, which we know as Sunday
will become for believers 'the Lord's Day'.
Very soon Christians will make a habit
of meeting on Sunday to acknowledge
and celebrate together the Risen Lord.

[19] It was late that Sunday evening, and the disciples were gathered together behind locked doors, because they were afraid of the Jewish authorities. Then Jesus came and stood among them. 'Peace be with you,' he said. [20] After saying this, he showed them his hands and side. The disciples were filled with joy at seeing the Lord. [21] Jesus said to them again, 'Peace be with you. As the Father sent me, so I send you.' [22] Then he breathed on them and said, 'Receive the Holy Spirit. [23] If you forgive people's sins, they are forgiven; if you do not forgive them, they are not forgiven.'

[24] One of the twelve disciples, Thomas (called the Twin), was not with them when Jesus came. [25] So the other disciples told him, 'We have seen the Lord!'

Thomas said to them, 'Unless I see the scars of the nails in his hands and put my finger on those scars and my hand in his side, I will not believe.'

[26] A week later the disciples were together again indoors, and Thomas was with them. The doors were locked, but Jesus came and stood among them and said, 'Peace be with you.' [27] Then he said to Thomas, 'Put your finger here, and look at my hands; then stretch out your hand and put it in

my side. Stop your doubting, and believe!'
²⁸Thomas answered him, 'My Lord and my God!'
²⁹Jesus said to him, 'Do you believe because you see me? How happy are those who believe without seeing me!'

John 20:19-29

From the apostle John we learn that the apostles have experienced something extraordinary that has changed everything for them.

The man standing in their midst is undoubtedly the Jesus whom they know, whom they followed and to whom they listened . . . and yet he is quite different. He comes in unannounced while the doors and windows are bolted. His body is no longer solid and substantial. Yet without a doubt it is his body, the body which was nailed to the cross and which still bears the marks of the nails. Jesus is completely transformed, as he was that day on the mountainside (chapter 19). It is the same person, but living fully now the life of God.

Normally a risen body cannot be seen. It is by an extraordinary favour that the apostles are allowed to see and hear Christ living his new life, and even, as Thomas did, to touch his hands and his side. This experience was necessary in order that faith should be born in the hearts of the disciples and that they should recognize in Jesus their 'Lord and their God'. 'Do you believe because you see me?' Jesus said to Thomas. 'How happy are those who believe without seeing me.' That is how Christians in future must believe in Jesus: without seeing him, but trusting completely the testimony of those who have seen him.

To enable the apostles to become his witnesses, Jesus fills them with his Spirit. When he breathes over them it is the Holy Spirit he is breathing into them, the Spirit who formed him inside the body of his mother Mary (see chapter 1), the Spirit who set him apart to spread the good news (chapter 5). The apostles too will be filled with and led by the Holy Spirit, for they have been commissioned to continue Jesus' work. It is in the Spirit's name that they will proclaim the mercy of God and reconcile men and women with the Father.

Detail from the reredos of the Pieta of Avignon (France).

Any day of the week you are happy to meet with friends; sometimes there is a birthday to celebrate. For Christians, every Sunday is the anniversary of Jesus' resurrection. It is a feast day and we come together to meet Jesus, to celebrate the risen Jesus in whom we believe. When you go to church, open your heart to him, in faith. To you too Jesus says: 'Stop your doubting and believe.'

28

To the ends of the earth

Following the gospels in the New Testament are the Acts of the Apostles.
Written by St Luke, this book is a sequel to his gospel.
First of all, it tells how the risen Jesus
shows his apostles what they must do when he is gone.
Then it describes the beginnings of the Church
and shows how, thanks to the Holy Spirit,
the Church spread from Jerusalem to Rome,
preaching the resurrection of Christ.

> [4] And when they came together, he gave them this order: 'Do not leave Jerusalem, but wait for the gift I told you about, the gift my Father promised. [5] John baptized with water, but in a few days you will be baptized with the Holy Spirit.'
>
> [6] When the apostles met together with Jesus, they asked him, 'Lord, will you at this time give the Kingdom back to Israel?'
>
> [7] Jesus said to them, 'The times and occasions are set by my Father's own authority, and it is not for you to know when they will be. [8] But when the Holy Spirit comes upon you, you will be filled with power and you will be witnesses for me in Jerusalem, in all Judaea and Samaria, and to the ends of the earth.' [9] After saying this, he was taken up to heaven as they watched him, and a cloud hid him from their sight.

Acts 1:4-9

The coming of the Spirit

St John tells us that Jesus gave the Holy Spirit to his apostles on the evening of the day he rose from the dead. In this passage from the Acts of the Apostles Jesus promises that the Holy Spirit will come later, 'in a few days'. The Spirit will in fact descend on the apostles on the day of Pentecost and transform them. Does the Spirit come more than once, then?

Yes indeed! The Spirit comes continually . . . and this is still true. It is the Holy Spirit whom we receive at our baptism, who is established within us when we are confirmed. But we pray to the Spirit at many other times in our lives: the Spirit penetrates our being and helps us to live as better witnesses to Jesus.

The scene described here is known as 'the Ascension', because the text says that Jesus was 'taken up' and disappeared into a cloud. This is an image, used to express the truth that Jesus, identified from now on with the life and glory of God, is no longer visible on earth. The 'heaven' into which Jesus is welcomed is the intimacy of his Father, not an extra-terrestrial place.

This is the last time that Jesus appears to the apostles with his risen human body. He makes them a promise and gives them a mission.

The mission: to be his witnesses. That is, to make known all they have seen and heard, and above all the fact that although Jesus was put to death he rose again and is still alive. They will have to proclaim this extraordinary news in Jerusalem, to the rest of the Jewish people, to the Samaritans — those despised neighbours of theirs — and to all peoples, even 'to the ends of the earth'. From the first the mission of the Church has been universal, since the salvation brought by Jesus Christ is for all men and women.

The promise is given to make the mission possible. For the task given by Jesus to the apostles far exceeds their capabilities. The Lord promises to endow those he sends with a mysterious power, the power of the Holy Spirit, who will come down upon them as it came down upon Jesus on the day of his baptism. It is the Holy Spirit who will enlighten, strengthen and guide the messengers of the gospel. From start to finish, what the Acts of the Apostles in fact describe are the 'acts of the Holy Spirit'; working in an amazing way within the Church.

When, after the Ascension, the apostles find themselves alone, deprived of the visible presence of Jesus, they withdraw to a house in Jerusalem. For ten days, praying in the company of Mary, they wait for the coming of the promised Spirit.

Do you know what a missionary is?
After twenty centuries are there still countries
where the gospel has not yet been proclaimed?
Do you know any children who have never heard of Jesus?

29

Filled with the Holy Spirit

The word 'Pentecost' is from a Greek word meaning 'fiftieth': Pentecost is the fiftieth day after the Passover. For Jews it is a great feast celebrating the giving of the Law to Moses on Sinai, and the sealing of the covenant between God and the people of Israel. When this feast came round, many Jews, who lived in the various provinces of the Roman Empire, would come to Jerusalem to pray in the Temple.

¹When the day of Pentecost came, all the believers were gathered together in one place. ²Suddenly there was a noise from the sky which sounded like a strong wind blowing, and it filled the whole house where they were sitting. ³Then they saw what looked like tongues of fire which spread out and touched each person there. ⁴They were all filled with the Holy Spirit and began to talk in other languages, as the Spirit enabled them to speak.

⁵There were Jews living in Jerusalem, religious men who had come from every country in the world. ⁶When they heard this noise, a large crowd gathered. They were all excited, because each one of them heard the believers speaking in his own language. ⁷In amazement and wonder they exclaimed, 'These people who are talking like this are Galileans! ⁸How is it, then, that all of us hear them speaking in our own native languages? ⁹We are . . . from Mesopotamia, Judaea, . . . ¹⁰from Egypt and the regions of Libya near Cyrene. Some of us are from Rome, ¹¹both Jews and Gentiles converted to Judaism, and some of us are from Crete and Arabia — yet all of us hear them speaking in our own languages about the great things that God has done!' ¹²Amazed and confused, they kept asking each other, 'What does this mean?'

¹³But others made fun of the believers, saying, 'These people are drunk!'

¹⁴Then Peter stood up with the other eleven apostles and in a loud voice began to speak to the crowd: 'Fellow-Jews and all of you who live in Jerusalem, listen to me and let me tell you what this means. ¹⁵These people are not drunk, as you suppose; it is only nine o'clock in the morning. ¹⁶Instead, this is what the prophet Joel spoke about:
¹⁷"This is what I will do in the last days, God says:
   I will pour out my Spirit on everyone.
   Your sons and daughters will proclaim my message;
     your young men will see visions,
     and your old men will have dreams.
¹⁸Yes, even on my servants, both men and women,
   I will pour out my Spirit in those days,
   and they will proclaim my message." . . .

²²'Listen to these words, fellow-Israelites! Jesus of Nazareth was a man whose divine authority was clearly proven to you by all the miracles and wonders which God performed through him. You yourselves know this, for it happened here among you. ²³In accordance with his own plan God had already decided that Jesus would be handed over to you; and you killed him by letting sinful men crucify him. ²⁴But God raised him from death, setting him free from its power. . . . ³²We are all witnesses to this fact. . . . ³⁶'All the people of Israel, then, are to know for sure that this Jesus, whom you crucified, is the one that God has made Lord and Messiah!'

³⁷When the people heard this, they were deeply troubled and said to Peter and the other apostles, 'What shall we do, brothers?'

³⁸Peter said to them, 'Each one of you must turn away from his sins and be baptized in the name of Jesus Christ, so that your sins will be forgiven; and you will receive God's gift, the Holy Spirit.'

Acts 2

Pentecost is also the fulfilment of the promise Jesus made to his apostles.

— The Holy Spirit comes as a driving force.

— The apostles bear witness to the risen Christ.

— The Church is born, open from the first to men and women from all countries.

In talking about the Holy Spirit, this account makes use of various images: the rushing wind, the fire, the many tongues (languages), the delirious joy that looks like drunkenness.... From these images the Holy Spirit emerges as elusive like the wind, powerful like the storm, resplendent like fire. Speaking to all peoples and to each individual in their own language, the Spirit is the source of fervour, of joy and of enthusiasm. This passage demonstrates above all the extraordinary power of the Holy Spirit: transforming the Twelve, who until then were hesitant and fearful, into intrepid men who speak to the crowd with conviction.

Peter's speech — of which we have a resumé here — proclaims what all the apostles will proclaim about Jesus wherever they go. That Jesus, who was crucified and who died, has been raised up by God and 'seated at his right hand' (which means 'treated as his equal'). The apostles present themselves as witnesses of Jesus' resurrection. And on the basis of that central event they profess their faith in Jesus. He is the 'Christ', that is, the Messiah promised to Israel; he is the 'Lord', that is, God. It is thanks to him that the Holy Spirit is now given to transform people's hearts.

The Church is born of the witness and teaching of the apostles. All those who believe ask for baptism, thus entering into the community of Jesus' disciples. They are granted forgiveness for their sins; in receiving the Spirit they become children of God. Those listening to Peter come from many different countries. Whether Jewish or pagan by birth, they all believe in the God of Israel, the only true God. But they speak the language of their own country. They represent all peoples. From the very first day the Church, led by the Holy Spirit, opens itself to people from all over the world: it is universal.

One day you will be confirmed (you may be already).
Then the Holy Spirit will give you the courage and strength to live and to witness to your faith in the risen Jesus.

With believers throughout the world you can say this prayer:
Come Holy Spirit,
fill the hearts of all people,
and light in them the fire of your love.

30

They shared all they had

On the day of Pentecost
the Church is born in Jerusalem.
And it is there too
that it will begin to grow and expand.
At this stage all is fresh and new,
just as the Holy Spirit made it.
The Church is not yet disfigured
by the sins of its members.
Or at least, only good is remembered of it.
This first community of Jesus' disciples
remains for all time a model and a challenge.
By observing their way of life,
the Church, as the centuries go by,
rediscovers what God is asking of it, today.

⁴¹Many of them believed his message and were baptized, and about three thousand people were added to the group that day. ⁴²They spent their time in learning from the apostles, taking part in the fellowship, and sharing in the fellowship meals and the prayers.

⁴³Many miracles and wonders were being done through the apostles, and everyone was filled with awe. ⁴⁴All the believers continued together in close fellowship and shared their belongings with one another. ⁴⁵They would sell their property and possessions, and distribute the money among all, according to what each one needed. ⁴⁶Day after day they met as a group in the Temple, and they had their meals together in their homes, eating with glad and humble hearts, ⁴⁷praising God, and enjoying the good will of all the people. And every day the Lord added to their group those who were being saved.

Acts 2:41-47

The first Christians form a community. They share all they have.

— They share **their faith** in the Lord Jesus. To nourish this faith they listen attentively as the apostles teach them what Jesus said and did.

— They share **their prayer.** Living in Jerusalem and knowing that they belong to the people of God, they continue to go to the Temple to pray, following Jesus' example. And they also pray in their own homes. Their prayer is joyful, full of praise and thanksgiving.

— They share **their daily lives.** They regard themselves as brothers and sisters and do not want there to be rich and poor among them. So they share their money. And out of friendship they often eat together. Other people say of them: 'See how they love one another!'

— In this community of brothers and sisters, the most important time is when, as believers, they **'break bread'** together. The 'breaking of bread' is the first name Christians used to describe the 'Lord's Supper'. Because it unites each one of them to Christ, this act establishes a bond of communion between all the disciples of Jesus.

— The community as a whole bears **witness to its faith.** Like Jesus, the apostles perform signs. The love the Christians have for one another reveals the activity of the Holy Spirit in their hearts. The joy that radiates from the group attracts other people, and many ask to be admitted to the Church.

*Do you belong
to a Christian community?
Do you go . . .
to a catechism class . . .
or Sunday School?
Perhaps you go
to a church youth group
or sing in the choir.
Ask yourself:
by what signs
can people recognize you
and your companions
as disciples
and witnesses of Jesus.*

69

31 In the name of Jesus Christ

This passage completes the description of the Christian community in Jerusalem begun in the previous chapter.
We see Jesus' disciples going to the Temple to take part in the Jewish prayer.
We also see a miraculous sign being performed by the apostles.
On this occasion, as on the day of Pentecost,
Peter takes the lead: he acts as head of the Church.

¹One day Peter and John went to the Temple at three o'clock in the afternoon, the hour for prayer. ²There at the Beautiful Gate, as it was called, was a man who had been lame all his life. Every day he was carried to the gate to beg for money from the people who were going into the Temple. ³When he saw Peter and John going in, he begged them to give him something. ⁴They looked straight at him, and Peter said, 'Look at us!' ⁵So he looked at them, expecting to get something from them. ⁶But Peter said to him, 'I have no money at all, but I give you what I have: in the name of Jesus Christ of Nazareth I order you to get up and walk!' ⁷Then he took him by his right hand and helped him up. At once the man's feet and ankles became strong; ⁸he jumped up, stood on his feet, and started walking around.

The Beautiful Gate (Jerusalem).

> Then he went into the Temple with them, walking and jumping and praising God. ⁹The people there saw him walking and praising God, ¹⁰and when they recognized him as the beggar who had sat at the Beautiful Gate, they were all surprised and amazed at what had happened to him.
>
> ¹¹As the man held on to Peter and John in Solomon's Porch, as it was called, the people were amazed and ran to them. ¹²When Peter saw the people, he said to them, 'Fellow-Israelites, why are you surprised at this, and why do you stare at us? Do you think it was by means of our own power or godliness that we made this man walk? ¹³The God of Abraham, Isaac, and Jacob, the God of our ancestors, has given divine glory to his Servant Jesus. But you handed him over to the authorities.... ¹⁵You killed the one who leads to life, but God raised him from death — and we are witnesses to this. ¹⁶It was the power of his name that gave strength to this lame man. What you see and know was done by faith in his name; it was faith in Jesus that has made him well, as you can all see.'
>
> 4 Peter and John were still speaking to the people when some priests, the officer in charge of the temple guards, and some Sadducees arrived. ²They were annoyed because the two apostles were teaching the people that Jesus had risen from death, which proved that the dead will rise to life ³So they arrested them and put them in jail until the next day.

Acts 3:1-16; 4:1-3

Jesus frequently cured sick people: the blind, the deaf, the paralysed . . . now Peter cures a lame man with the same end in view: that is, to show that the kingdom of God — salvation — has come. But Peter does not act through his own power. He tells the man that Jesus is going to cure him. In this way he affirms that Jesus is still alive, that he is present and active, and that he is truly the one through whom 'God saves' (which is what the name Jesus signifies). Through Peter, Jesus is manifesting his loving-kindness and his power.

When they see the miracle, the crowd, who have come to pray, gather round the apostles. Peter then speaks, much as he did on the day of Pentecost: 'We are witnesses to the resurrection of Jesus.' It is their faith in the risen Jesus that has cured this lame man. Faith in him who saves the human race. This is the good news, which the apostles will go on and on repeating.

By proclaiming the resurrection of Jesus, Peter and John provoke the anger of members of the Sanhedrin, the Council of the Jews which had sought the condemnation of Jesus.

The two disciples are immediately arrested and put into prison. On several occasions the apostles will be threatened like this, imprisoned and beaten. From the very beginning of its existence, the Church, in carrying out its mission, has met with opposition. Like Jesus, the Church preaches salvation, and people want to silence it as they tried to silence him. The preaching of the gospel is based on witness, frequently relies on signs and sometimes involves persecution.

It is unlikely you have 'silver or gold' or that you will be asked to cure . . . so in Jesus' name, what can you give others?

32 Lord Jesus receive my spirit

Six or seven years after Pentecost,
there are many disciples of Jesus
in Jerusalem.
Their numbers are posing problems,
for aspects of daily life
like sharing money and meals,
or helping the sick and the widows.
The twelve apostles cannot do everything.
So they decide to appoint seven men — to
be known as 'deacons' or 'helpers' — to
assist them.
The first of these is Stephen,
who as well as serving the community,
is involved heart and soul in proclaiming
the death and resurrection of Jesus.

⁸**Stephen, a man richly blessed by God and full of power, performed great miracles and wonders among the people.** ⁹**But he was opposed by some men who were members of the synagogue of the Freedmen (as it was called), which included Jews from Cyrene and Alexandria. They and other Jews from the provinces of Cilicia and Asia started arguing with Stephen.** ¹⁰**But the Spirit gave Stephen such wisdom that when he spoke, they could not refute him.** ¹¹**So they bribed some men to say, 'We heard him speaking against Moses and against God!'** ¹²**In this way they stirred up the people, the elders, and the teachers of the Law. They seized Stephen and took him before the Council.** ¹³**Then they brought in some men to tell lies about him. 'This man,' they said, 'is always talking against our sacred Temple and the Law of Moses.** ¹⁴**We heard him say that**

The martyrdom of St Stephen, Twelfth century stained glass window. Mans Cathedral.

this Jesus of Nazareth will tear down the Temple and change all the customs which have come down to us from Moses!' ¹⁵All those sitting in the Council fixed their eyes on Stephen and saw that his face looked like the face of an angel. . . .

⁵⁵Stephen, full of the Holy Spirit, looked up to heaven and saw God's glory and Jesus standing at the right-hand side of God. ⁵⁶'Look!' he said. 'I see heaven opened and the Son of Man standing at the right-hand side of God!'

⁵⁷With a loud cry the members of the Council covered their ears with their hands. Then they all rushed at him at once, ⁵⁸threw him out of the city, and stoned him. The witnesses left their cloaks in the care of a young man named Saul. ⁵⁹They kept on stoning Stephen as he called out to the Lord, 'Lord Jesus, receive my spirit!' ⁶⁰He knelt down and cried out in a loud voice, 'Lord! Do not remember this sin against them!' He said this and died.

8 And Saul approved of his murder.

Acts 6 and 8

— There are still martyrs today. Do you know where?
— One can witness to Jesus through one's words, one's life or one's death. Do you know any true Christian witnesses? Who are they? What do they do?

Stephen is led by the Holy Spirit who fills him with wisdom and power (the text insists on this, repeating it twice). It is the Holy Spirit who enables Stephen to become a witness to Jesus: Lord and Christ. What began at Pentecost continues in the Church.

Brought before the Sanhedrin, Stephen declares that he sees Jesus in heaven 'standing at God's right side'; Stephen is thus affirming that Jesus is equal to God, and this affirmation leads to his being condemned to death for blasphemy. Jesus, at his trial, was accused and condemned for the same reason.

In several respects the paths that led to their deaths are similar. In his account of the passion of Christ, St Luke passes on to us several things Jesus said that are not found in St Mark's gospel. Just after his executioners have nailed him to the cross, Jesus prays: 'Forgive them, Father! They don't know what they are doing.' And just before he dies: 'Father, in your hands I place my spirit' — that is, 'I give you my life.' In the same way, Stephen asks God to pardon his executioners. And just as Jesus commended his spirit to the Father, so Stephen commends his to Jesus his 'Lord', thus showing that he acknowledges him as God. In this way Stephen shows himself to be the disciple who follows his master even in his death.

Jesus died because he claimed to be the Messiah and the Son of God. Stephen died because he proclaimed that Jesus had risen from the dead, that he was the Saviour, and the Son of God. Both died bearing witness to the truth. Stephen is the first Christian martyr.

In Greek, the word 'martyr' means 'witness'. The Christian martyrs are those who have borne witness to their faith right to the end, in spite of threats, persecution and torture. Throughout the centuries there have always been martyrs. The martyrs united their own deaths to the death of Jesus. And their blood has been described as 'the seed of the Church'.

For the first time here, Saul is mentioned. He will reappear frequently in what follows. Later he will be called Paul. He will play a very important role in the Church.

33   *I am Jesus whom you persecute*

Saul was born in Tarsus, in what is now Turkey.
He speaks Greek, like all the inhabitants
of the region at that time.
His father is a pharisee, that is, a Jew
who observes faithfully the Law of the covenant.
He wants his son to become a good pharisee,
well instructed in the Law,
so Saul is sent to study in Jerusalem.
Saul is a pupil of one of the great masters
and in time becomes a professor himself.
He is about ten years younger than Jesus.
When he arrives in Jerusalem
Jesus has already been crucified.
The Church is expanding.
After the condemnation of Stephen,
Saul throws himself heart and soul
into opposing the followers of Christ,
who, as he sees it, disturb and threaten
the religion of Israel.

¹In the meantime Saul kept up his violent threats of murder against the followers of the Lord. He went to the High Priest ²and asked for letters of introduction to the synagogues in Damascus, so that if he should find there any followers of the Way of the Lord, he would be able to arrest them, both men and women, and bring them back to Jerusalem.
³As Saul was coming near the city of Damascus, suddenly a light from the sky flashed round him. ⁴He fell to the ground and heard a voice saying to him, 'Saul, Saul! Why do you persecute me?' ⁵'Who are you, Lord?' he asked. 'I am Jesus, whom you persecute,' the voice said. ⁶'But get up and go into the city, where you will be told what you must do.'
⁷The men who were travelling with Saul had stopped, not saying a word; they heard the voice but could not see anyone. ⁸Saul got up from the ground and opened his eyes, but could not see a thing. So they took him by the hand and led him into Damascus. ⁹For three days he was not able to see, and during that time he did not eat or drink

St Paul at the house of Ananias in Damascus. Thirteenth century stained glass window. Rouen Cathedral.

anything. ¹⁰There was a Christian in Damascus named Ananias. He had a vision, in which the Lord said to him, 'Ananias!' 'Here I am, Lord,' he answered. ¹¹The Lord said to him, 'Get ready and go to Straight Street, and at the house of Judas ask for a man from Tarsus named Saul. He is praying, ¹²and in a vision he has seen a man named Ananias come in and place his hands on him so that he might see again.' . . .

¹⁷So Ananias went, entered the house where Saul was, and placed his hands on him. 'Brother Saul,' he said, 'the Lord has sent me — Jesus himself, who appeared to you on the road as you were coming here. He sent me so that you might see again and be filled with the Holy Spirit.' ¹⁸At once something like fish scales fell from Saul's eyes, and he was able to see again. He stood up and was baptized; ¹⁹and after he had eaten, his strength came back.

Saul stayed for a few days with the believers in Damascus. ²⁰He went straight to the synagogues and began to preach that Jesus was the Son of God.

Acts 9:1-12 . 17-20

On the road near Damascus, Saul is abruptly thrown from his horse and blinded by the light of God. Jesus is there and speaks to him. Then Saul realises two things for certain. The first is that Jesus is truly alive, risen. And the second is that anyone who persecutes the disciples of Jesus, is in fact persecuting Jesus himself. Between Christ and the community of believers there is a real, profound and mysterious union.

Jesus sends Saul along to the Church so that he can be rescued from his darkness and fully enlightened by the Holy Spirit. First of all, Saul, who is still blind, fasts and prays for three days. Next Ananias, a disciple of Christ living in Damascus, receives him into the community by laying hands on him and baptizing him. Saul is cured. His eyes once again see the light of day and his spirit is open to faith.

Usually this event is known as 'the conversion of Saul'. In reality, however, Saul was not 'converted', that is to say he did not 'turn back' towards Christ. It was Christ who took hold of him. Jesus harnessed to his service the faith and the burning enthusiasm of this young pharisee who wanted with all the power of his being to do the will of God.

Immediately after his baptism, Saul proclaims to the Jews of Damascus that he believes in Jesus, the Messiah and Son of God. Later, after several years spent in solitude and silence, he will become a tireless apostle, travelling all over the world to preach the gospel.

Lord Jesus
you have given me your life
through my baptism.
Continue to give me life,
open my eyes,
and fill me with your light.

[34] Sent by the Holy Spirit

Antioch was a very large town. Thanks to the nearby port of Seleucis it was open to the Mediterranean and therefore to the entire Empire. It was the capital of the Roman province of Syria, of which Palestine was a part. This town was quickly to become an important centre for the Church.

[19] Some of the believers who were scattered by the persecution which took place when Stephen was killed went as far as Phoenicia, Cyprus, and Antioch, telling the message to Jews only. [20] But other believers, men from Cyprus and Cyrene, went to Antioch and proclaimed the message to Gentiles also, telling them the Good News about the Lord Jesus. [21] The Lord's power was with them, and a great number of people believed and turned to the Lord.

[22] The news about this reached the church in Jerusalem, so they sent Barnabas to Antioch. . . .

[25] Then Barnabas went to Tarsus to look for Saul. [26] When he found him, he took him to Antioch, and for a whole year the two met with the people of the church and taught a large group. It was at Antioch that the believers were first called Christians. . . .

13 In the church at Antioch there were some prophets and teachers: Barnabas, Simeon (called the Black), Lucius (from Cyrene), Manaen (who had been brought up with Herod the governor), and Saul. [2] While they were serving the Lord and fasting, the Holy Spirit said to them, 'Set apart for me Barnabas and Saul, to do the work to which I have called them.'

[3] They fasted and prayed, placed their hands on them, and sent them off. [4] Having been sent by the Holy Spirit, Barnabas and Saul went to Seleucia and sailed from there to the island of Cyprus.

Acts 11 and 13

The laying on of hands

To lay hands on someone is to place one's hands on that person's head in order to take him or her under one's protection or to pass on the power of the Spirit.

It is a very ancient custom: many examples can be found in the Bible, long before Jesus was born.

Jesus himself often laid hands on people — on children, for example, or on the sick whom he cured.

In the Acts of the Apostles, the laying on of hands is always linked with the coming of the Holy Spirit: for the appointment of deacons, for baptism, when a cure takes place, or when someone is sent on a mission.

This gesture is still used today during the celebration of the sacraments.

Roman road probably taken by St Paul. Antioch in Syria.

Lord, every day you call men and women
to go and pass on the good news
to those who do not know you yet.
Give them the power of your Spirit.
May your Spirit help me too, to witness to your love.
May your kingdom come.

This passage shows how, through events, the Holy Spirit is guiding the growth of the Church. The persecution which began with the murder of Stephen has persuaded a number of Jesus' followers to leave Jerusalem. Taking refuge in Antioch, they proclaim their faith and as a result a large and dynamic community develops. The townspeople, hearing them repeat continually the name of Christ, begin to call them 'Christians' ('Christianos' in Greek); the Christians are the followers of Jesus Christ.

Persecution has led to the expansion of the Church. For one thing, it is now established hundreds of kilometres away from Jerusalem. Secondly, in Antioch it has not only Jews but also converted pagans as members.

The Spirit supports this new community, keeping it in communion with the community in Jerusalem: Barnabas and Saul are the apostles' representatives for these new disciples of Christ, to some of whom the Holy Spirit gives the grace to be prophets or teachers.

— **The prophets** are people who, themselves in touch with God in their prayer, help their brothers and sisters to discover day by day what the Lord wants of them, and constantly call on them to be converted.

— **The doctors** are people who know the Bible well, and who are able to explain to Jesus' disciples those texts in which he was foretold under the old covenant.

One day, during a prayer meeting, the Holy Spirit, through the mouth of the prophets, asks the church in Antioch to give up Barnabas and Saul so that they can go further afield to preach the gospel. And so it happens that once their fellow Christians have laid hands on them, Barnabas and Saul are sent on their mission by the Holy Spirit.

[35] We will go to the Gentiles

Sent into the mission field by the Spirit,
Barnabas and Saul begin an impressive journey.
Travelling sometimes by ship,
sometimes on foot as part of a caravan,
they go from town to town
telling people about Jesus.
Eventually they reach Antioch in Pisidia
(not to be confused with Antioch in Syria)
among the mountains of Turkey.
On the way Saul has changed his Jewish name
for a Roman name, Paul;
and it is now he, not Barnabas,
who leads the expedition.

[13] Paul and his companions sailed from Paphos and came to Perga, a city in Pamphylia, where John Mark left them and went back to Jerusalem. [14] They went on from Perga and arrived in Antioch in Pisidia, and on the Sabbath they went into the synagogue and sat down. [15] After the reading from the Law of Moses and from the writings of the prophets, the officials of the synagogue sent them a message: 'Brothers, we want you to speak to the people if you have a message of encouragement for them.' [16] Paul stood up, motioned with his hand, and began to speak: ...
[23] 'It was Jesus, a descendant of David, whom God made the Saviour of the people of Israel, as he had promised. ...
[26] 'My fellow-Israelites, descendants of Abraham, and all Gentiles here who worship God: it is to us that this message of salvation has been sent! [27] For the people who live in Jerusalem and their leaders did not know that he is the Saviour, nor did they understand the words of the prophets that are read every Sabbath. Yet they made the

By this time the majority of the Jews had been living outside Palestine for several centuries, scattered throughout the countries that lie around the Mediterranean. In almost every town of the Roman Empire Jewish communities had grown up. Each had its own synagogue and its members observed faithfully the Law and the traditions of their people.

When they arrive in Antioch in Pisidia, Paul and Barnabas do as they have done in the other towns through which they have passed: on the Sabbath they attend the meeting in the synagogue. The fact that Paul is a doctor of the Law makes the Jewish leaders all the happier to receive them. They ask them to preach. The sermon Paul then addresses to his 'fellow Israelites, descendants of Abraham' (the Jews) and to 'all Gentiles here who worship God' (pagan converts to the Jewish religion) closely resembles Peter's sermon on the day of Pentecost. God, says Paul has fulfilled the promises made through the prophets, Jesus, a descendant of David, is the awaited Messiah; he was put to death by the authorities in Jerusalem; but God raised him up; he is the Lord. Those who believe in him receive forgiveness for their sins. That is the good news.

But for many Jews it is not the good news. According to them, this man Jesus, who died on a cross, cannot be the Messiah awaited by Israel. And despite what was said by the prophets (Paul quotes from Isaiah), they reject the idea that the Messiah promised to the Jewish people might also be sent to non-Jews. That is why they reject Paul and Barnabas.

The two men, obliged to leave the synagogue, turn to the pagans. Many, filled with admiration, believe their testimony. A Christian community is formed, made up principally of former pagans. This was something Paul and Barnabas, who wanted to preach the gospel to the Jews, had not foreseen. Events have made them change their plans: the Holy Spirit has forced their hand!

What is more, the Spirit also prompts them to continue their journey and found yet another new church. Having been driven out of Antioch in Pisidia, they travel 130 kilometres to Iconium. Once again, persecution, which sought to destroy the Church, has led to its expansion.

---

prophets' words come true by condemning Jesus. ²⁸And even though they could find no reason to pass the death sentence on him, they asked Pilate to have him put to death.... ³⁰But God raised him from death, ³¹and for many days he appeared to those who had travelled with him from Galilee to Jerusalem. They are now witnesses for him to the people of Israel. ³²⁻³³And we are here to bring the Good News to you: what God promised our ancestors he would do, he has now done for us, who are their descendants, by raising Jesus to life....

³⁸⁻³⁹We want you to know, my fellow-Israelites, that it is through Jesus that the message about forgiveness of sins is preached to you....

⁴⁴The next Sabbath nearly everyone in the town came to hear the word of the Lord. ⁴⁵When the Jews saw the crowds, they were filled with jealousy; they disputed what Paul was saying and insulted him. ⁴⁶But Paul and Barnabas spoke out even more boldly: 'It was necessary that the word of God should be spoken first to you. But since you reject it and do not consider yourselves worthy of eternal life, we will leave you and go to the Gentiles. ⁴⁷For this is the commandment that the Lord has given us:

"I have made you a light for the Gentiles, so that all the world may be saved."'

⁴⁸When the Gentiles heard this, they were glad and praised the Lord's message; and those who had been chosen for eternal life became believers.

⁴⁹The word of the Lord spread everywhere in that region. ⁵⁰But the Jews stirred up the leading men of the city and the Gentile women of high social standing who worshipped God. They started a persecution against Paul and Barnabas and threw them out of their region. ⁵²The believers in Antioch were full of joy and the Holy Spirit.

Acts 13

---

*How many Christians are there in your class?
How many Jews? How many Muslims?
And how many who believe
that God does not exist at all?*

*St Paul, teach us
to allow the Holy Spirit to lead us,
so that we, like you, will know
when to talk about Jesus Christ
and how to make him known.*

[36]

Do this in memory of me

During his second missionary journey
Paul went on from Turkey into Europe.
From 50 to 52 AD he stayed in Corinth in Greece,
where he founded a Christian community.
Four years later whilst undertaking a third journey,
Paul received messengers from Corinth.
The news they brought him
showed that all was not going well in the young church;
the Christians were divided amongst themselves.
So Paul wrote a letter to the Corinthians
urging them to be more faithful to the gospel.
If you cannot remember
what these letters (epistles)
from the apostles to the communities were,
reread page 5.

¹⁷In the following instructions, however, I do not praise you, because your meetings for worship actually do more harm than good. ¹⁸In the first place, I have been told that there are opposing groups in your meetings; and this I believe is partly true. . . . ²⁰When you meet together as a group, it is not the Lord's Supper that you eat. ²¹For as you eat, each one goes ahead with his own meal, so that some are hungry while others get drunk. ²²Haven't you got your own homes in which to eat and drink? Or would you rather despise the church of God and put to shame the people who are in need? What do you expect me to say to you about this? Shall I praise you? Of course I don't!

²³For I received from the Lord the teaching that I passed on to you: that the Lord Jesus, on the night he was betrayed, took a piece of bread, ²⁴gave thanks to God, broke it, and said, 'This is my body, which is for you. Do this in memory of me.' ²⁵In the same way, after the supper he took the cup and said, 'This cup is God's new covenant, sealed with my blood. Whenever you drink it, do so in memory of me.'

²⁶This means that every time you eat this bread and drink from this cup you proclaim the Lord's death until he comes.

I Corinthians 11:17-18 . 20-26

What we now call 'the Eucharist' the first Christians called 'the Lord's Supper'. It took place in the evening when the day's work was over. In Corinth they prepared for it by having a meal together. Everyone brought something to eat and they all shared with each other. It was a good way for the rich to help the poor and for the community to spend a friendly hour together.

Unfortunately, little by little the Corinthians fell into bad habits, the rich keeping for themselves the good food and fine wines, while the poor did not get enough to eat. Paul protested, because the meal had lost its spirit of fellowship and did nothing to prepare these Christians to celebrate the Lord's Supper. Quite the contrary, in fact!

So Paul reminded the Corinthians that the Lord's Supper is a reenactment of the last meal Jesus shared with his apostles on the evening before he died (see chapter 23). It was then that Jesus gave his body and blood and, having offered himself as food to his disciples (chapter 17), told them: 'Do this in memory of me.'

The apostles and disciples were faithful to Jesus' instruction, as Christians are today: when they come together the priest repeats the words and actions of Jesus. This is the Lord's Supper. It has also been called 'the breaking of bread' (chapter 30) because Jesus 'broke bread' and that was the sign by which the disciples at Emmaus recognised him. And finally, it has been given the name 'Eucharist', because Jesus 'gave thanks' to God — the Greek word *eucharistia* means 'thanksgiving': saying thank you.

In the Eucharist, Christians are united with Jesus in his passage to the Father. They allow themselves to be strengthened by his love. They are united among themselves like the members of a single body. And they voice their hope that one day they will see the face of the risen Lord.

Jesus said: 'Do this in memory of me.'
What is it that we do in memory of him? meet together?
listen to the gospel? receive his body?
learn to love one another?
When you go to church on Sunday, ask yourself
why you are going and what importance it has for you.

37 You must try to be like him

From 60 to 62 AD — about thirty years after the death of Jesus — Paul is in Rome, the capital of the Empire. For a long time he has wanted to come to this city, at that time the centre of the known world, to preach about Jesus Christ. He is not, however, on one of his great missionary journeys when he arrives there, but a prisoner, handcuffed and led by soldiers. Like Jesus he was accused by members of the Council in Jerusalem of stirring up rebellion; the governor imprisoned him and then sent him to Rome to be judged by the Emperor. While awaiting trial he writes several letters, including an important epistle to the church in Ephesus (in present-day Turkey), which he founded himself and which he visited on several occasions.

Inscription of St Peter and St Paul. Catacomb of St Sebastian. Rome.

¹I urge you, then — I who am a prisoner because I serve the Lord: live a life that measures up to the standard God set when he called you. ²Be always humble, gentle, and patient. Show your love by being tolerant with one another. ³Do your best to preserve the unity which the Spirit gives by means of the peace that binds you together. ⁴There is one body and one Spirit, just as there is one hope to which God has called you. ⁵There is one Lord, one faith, one baptism; ⁶there is one God and Father of all mankind, who is Lord of all, works through all, and is in all.

5 Since you are God's dear children, you must try to be like him. ²Your life must be controlled by love, just as Christ loved us and gave his life for us as a sweet-smelling offering and sacrifice that pleases God. . . .

⁸You yourselves used to be in the darkness, but since you have become the Lord's people, you are in the light. So you must live like people who belong to the light, ⁹for it is the light that brings a rich harvest of every kind of goodness, righteousness, and truth. ¹⁰Try to learn what pleases the Lord. . . .

¹⁵So be careful how you live. Don't live like ignorant people, but like wise people. . . . ¹⁷Don't be fools, then, but try to find out what the Lord wants you to do.

¹⁸. . . Be filled with the Spirit. ¹⁹Speak to one another with the words of psalms, hymns, and sacred songs; sing hymns and psalms to the Lord with praise in your hearts. ²⁰In the name of our Lord Jesus Christ, always give thanks for everything to God the Father.

Ephesians 4 and 5

The apostle Paul thinks that he may soon be condemned to death. He writes to the people he has brought to the faith, encouraging them to live according to that faith.

— Through faith and baptism Christians have been called to make up the family of God, the body of Christ. This is their joy, the source of their hope, the bond which unites them. They all have one and the same Father, they have all been brought together by Jesus. The same Spirit dwells within them all.

— To be a true child of God means following the example of Christ. It means loving as he loved, being like him a peacemaker and a forger of unity. It means living in fellowship with other people.

— In order to be closer to God their Father, Christians try to reflect his light. They ask the Holy Spirit to enlighten them more and more each day so that they can find out what God wants of them.

— The children of God are happy to be loved by their Father; they thank him for having called them to be his sons and daughters. They give thanks to God just as Jesus did. They gather together to express their joy in song and to proclaim the praises of the Lord.

Let us give glory
to the Father who loves us,
to his Son, Jesus Christ, the Lord,
to the Holy Spirit
who dwells in our hearts,
for ever and ever. Amen!

[38] Come, Lord Jesus

The Apocalypse is the last book of the Bible. It was written in about 95 AD during a great persecution which produced many martyrs. Much of the Apocalypse is difficult to understand. But it is a message of hope. It encourages Christians to stand fast, to remain faithful and trust in Jesus Christ. Having risen, Jesus is alive and present in his Church. He will never abandon those who believe in him, even if their enemies seem to be winning. 'Apocalypse' means 'Revelation'. The book of the Apocalypse upholds the faith of Christians by giving them a glimpse of life with God in the new world which will replace the present one.

> [1] Then I saw a new heaven and a new earth. The first heaven and the first earth disappeared, and the sea vanished. [2] And I saw the Holy City, the new Jerusalem, coming down out of heaven from God, prepared and ready, like a bride dressed to meet her husband. [3] I heard a loud voice speaking from the throne: 'Now God's home is with mankind! He will live with them, and they shall be his people. God himself will be with them, and he will be their God. [4] He will wipe away all tears from their eyes. There will be no more death, no more grief or crying or pain. The old things have disappeared.'
>
> [5] Then the one who sits on the throne said, 'And now I make all things new!'
>
> *Reveiation 21:1-5*

The heavenly Jerusalem. *Liber floridus* of Lambert.
Flemish, fifteenth century. Musee Condé. Chantilly.

The Apocalypse, written for believers undergoing severe trials, expresses powerfully the contrast between their present life and the life to come.

Here on earth human beings suffer from the effects of sickness, famine and war. People cause one another unhappiness through their acts of violence and injustice. Christians are persecuted because of their faith. All of us are familiar with fatigue, pain, fear . . . and in the end we all die. It is in the midst of this world that the Church of Jesus Christ exists, thus continuing the passion of the Lord. But after the passion will come the resurrection, of each individual and of the world as a whole.

One day there will no longer be any tears, or grief, or sadness or death. On that day Christ will return with power, to make joy and love triumphant at last and to establish the kingdom of God among all people for all time. This will be the end of the world as we know it. Risen like Jesus and with Jesus, we will find ourselves living with him in the 'new heaven and new earth', where we will see God as he sees us and where his love will fill us with happiness.

This future, promised to all human beings, is the great source of hope for Christians.

*Following the example
of the first Christians,
we sing:*

*Glory be to you,
once dead and now alive,
our Saviour and our God.
Come Lord Jesus!*

85

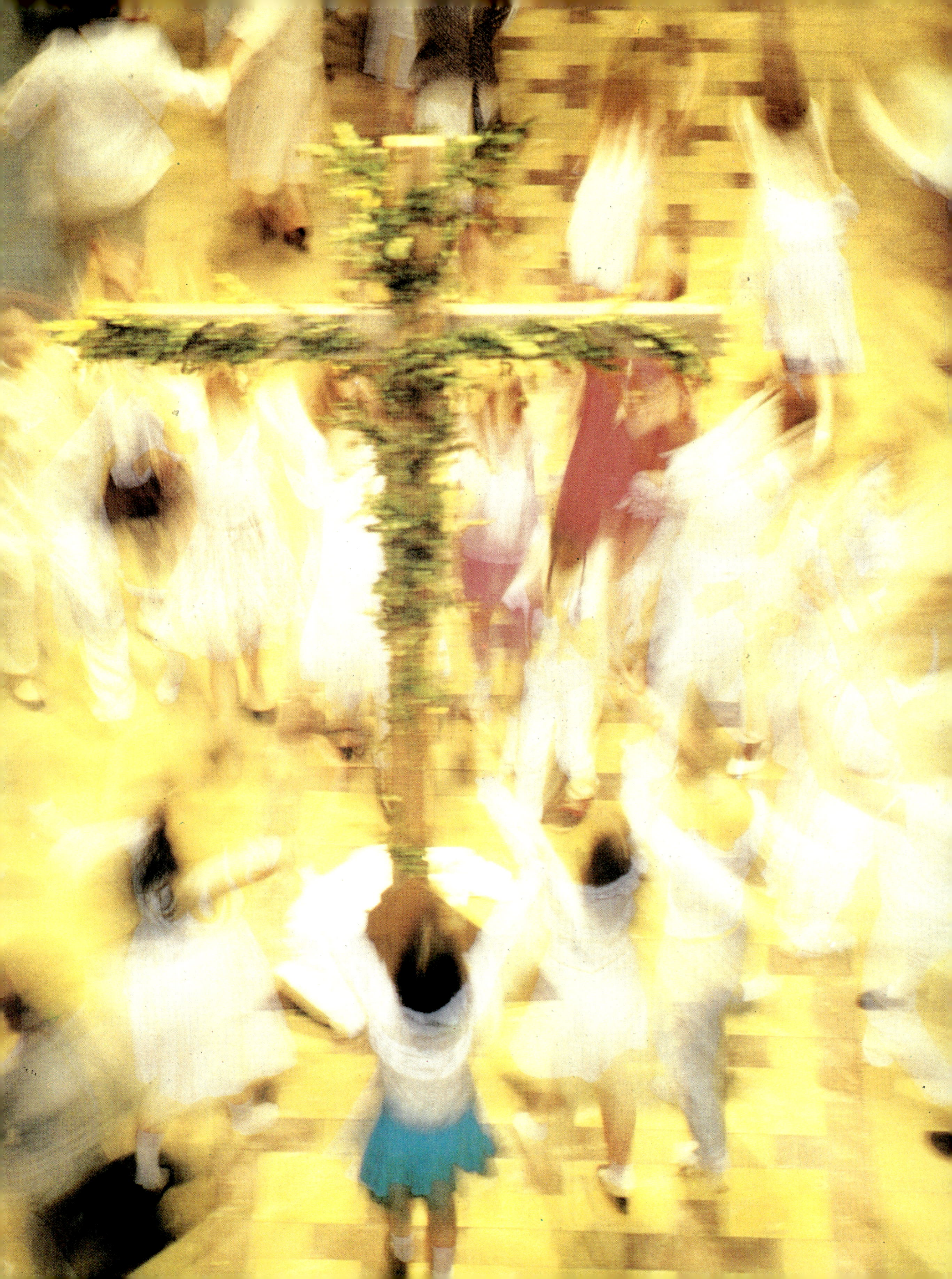

That our joy may be complete

We write to you about the Word of life, which has existed from the very beginning. We have heard it, and we have seen it with our eyes; yes, we have seen it and our hands have touched it. When this life became visible, we saw it; so we speak of it and tell you about the eternal life which was with the Father and was made known to us. What we have seen and heard we announce to you also, so that you will join with us in the fellowship that we have with the Father and with his son Jesus Christ. We write this in order that our joy may be complete.

I John 1:1-4